Tennessee Williams was born in 1911 in Columbus, Mississippi, where his grandfather was the episcopal clergyman. When his father, a travelling salesman, moved with his family to St Louis some years later, both he and his sister found it impossible to settle down to city life. He entered college during the Depression and left after a couple of years to take a clerical job in a shoe company. He stayed there for two years, spending the evenings writing. He entered the University of Iowa in 1938 and completed his course, at the same time holding a large number of part-time jobs of great diversity. He received a Rockefeller Fellowship in 1940 for his play *Battle of Angels*, and he won the Pulitzer Prize in 1948 and 1955. Among his many other plays Penguin have published *A Streetcar Named Desire* (1947), *Summer and Smoke* (1948), *The Rose Tattoo* (1951), *Camino Real* (1953), *Cat on a Hot Tin Roof* (1955), *Baby Doll* (1957), *Orpheus Descending* (1957), *Something Unspoken* (1958), *Suddenly Last Summer* (1958), *Sweet Bird of Youth* (1959), *Period of Adjustment* (1960), *The Night of the Iguana* (1961), *The Milk Train Doesn't Stop Here Anymore* (1963; revised 1964) and *Small Craft Warnings* (1972).

Tennessee Williams died in 1983.

Peter Shaffer has written of Tennessee Williams: 'He was a born dramatist as few are ever born. Whatever he put on paper, superb or superfluous, glorious or gaudy, could not fail to be electrifyingly actable. He could not write a dull scene . . . Tennessee Williams will live as long as drama itself.'

TENNESSEE WILLIAMS

The
Glass Menagerie

EDITED BY
E. MARTIN BROWNE

PENGUIN BOOKS
in association with
Martin Secker & Warburg Ltd

PENGUIN BOOKS

Published by the Penguin Group
Penguin Books Ltd, 27 Wrights Lane, London W8 5TZ, England
Penguin Putnam Inc., 375 Hudson Street, New York, New York 10014, USA
Penguin Books Australia Ltd, Ringwood, Victoria, Australia
Penguin Books Canada Ltd, 10 Alcorn Avenue, Toronto, Ontario, Canada M4V 3B2
Penguin Books (NZ) Ltd, Private Bag 102902, NSMC, Auckland, New Zealand

Penguin Books Ltd, Registered Offices: Harmondsworth, Middlesex, England

Published together with *A Streetcar Named Desire* in Penguin Books 1959
Reprinted with *Sweet Bird of Youth* 1962
This separate edition published 1988
18

Printed in England by Clays Ltd, St Ives plc
Set in Baskerville

CONTENTS

THE CHARACTERS

AMANDA WINGFIELD [*the mother*]: A little woman of great but confused vitality clinging frantically to another time and place. Her characterization must be carefully created, not copied from type. She is not paranoiac, but her life is paranoia. There is much to admire in Amanda, and as much to love and pity as there is to laugh at. Certainly she has endurance and a kind of heroism, and though her foolishness makes her unwittingly cruel at times, there is tenderness in her slight person.

LAURA WINGFIELD [*her daughter*]: Amanda, having failed to establish contact with reality, continues to live vitally in her illusions, but Laura's situation is even graver. A childhood illness has left her crippled, one leg slightly shorter than the other, and held in a brace. This defect need not be more than suggested on the stage. Stemming from this, Laura's separation increases till she is like a piece of her own glass collection, too exquisitely fragile to move from the shelf.

TOM WINGFIELD [*her son, and the narrator of the play*]: A poet with a job in a warehouse. His nature is not remorseless, but to escape from a trap he has to act without pity.

JIM O'CONNOR [*the gentleman caller*]: A nice, ordinary, young man.

PRODUCTION NOTES

Being a 'memory play', *The Glass Menagerie* can be presented with unusual freedom from convention. Because of its considerably delicate or tenuous material, atmospheric touches and subtleties of direction play a particularly important part. Expressionism and all other unconventional techniques in drama have only one valid aim, and that is a closer approach to truth. When a play employs unconventional techniques, it is not, or certainly shouldn't be, trying to escape its responsibility of dealing with reality, or interpreting experience, but is actually or should be attempting to find a closer approach, a more penetrating and vivid expression of things as they are. The straight realistic play with its genuine frigidaire and authentic ice-cubes, its characters that speak exactly as its audience speaks, corresponds to the academic landscape and has the same virtue of a photographic likeness. Everyone should know nowadays the unimportance of the photographic in art: that truth, life, or reality is an organic thing which the poetic imagination can represent or suggest, in essence, only through transformation, through changing into other forms than those which were merely present in appearance.

These remarks are not meant as a preface only to this particular play. They have to do with a conception of a new, plastic theatre which must take the place of the exhausted theatre of realistic conventions if the theatre is to resume vitality as a part of our culture.

THE SCREEN DEVICE

There is *only one important difference between the original and acting version of the play* and that is the *omission* in the latter of the device which I tentatively included in my *original* script. This device was the use of a screen on which were projected magic-lantern slides bearing images or titles. I do not regret the omission of this device from the present Broadway production. The extraordinary power of Miss Taylor's performance made it suitable to have the utmost simplicity in the physical production. But I think it may be interesting to some readers to see how this device was conceived. So I am putting it into the published manuscript. These images and legends, projected from behind, were cast on a section of wall between the front room and the dining-room areas, which should be indistinguishable from the rest when not in use.

The purpose of this will probably be apparent. It is to give accent to certain values in each scene. Each scene contains a particular point (or several) which is structurally the most important. In an episodic play, such as this, the basic structure or narrative line may be obscured from the audience; the effect may seem fragmentary rather than architectural. This may not be the fault of the play so much as a lack of attention in the audience. The legend or image upon the screen will strengthen the effect of what is merely illusion in the writing and allow the primary point to be made more simply and lightly than if the entire responsibility were on the spoken lines. Aside from this structural value, I think the screen will have a definite emotional appeal, less definable but just as important. An imaginative producer or director may invent many other uses for this device than those indicated in the present script. In fact the possibilities of the device seem much larger to me than the instance of this play can possibly utilize.

THE MUSIC

Another extra-literary accent in this play is provided by the use of music. A single recurring tune, 'The Glass Menagerie', is used to give emotional emphasis to suitable passages. This tune is like circus music, not when you are on the grounds or in the immediate vicinity of the parade, but when you are at some distance and very likely thinking of something else. It seems under those circumstances to continue almost interminably and it weaves in and out of your preoccupied consciousness; then it is the lightest, most delicate music in the world and perhaps the saddest. It expresses the surface vivacity of life with the underlying strain of immutable and inexpressible sorrow. When you look at a piece of delicately spun glass you think of two things: how beautiful it is and how easily it can be broken. Both of those ideas should be woven into the recurring tune, which dips in and out of the play as if it were carried on a wind that changes. It serves as a thread of connexion and allusion between the narrator with his separate point in time and space and the subject of his story. Between each episode it returns as reference to the emotion, nostalgia, which is the first condition of the play. It is primarily LAURA's music and therefore comes out most clearly when the play focuses upon her and the lovely fragility of glass which is her image.

THE LIGHTING

The lighting in the play is not realistic. In keeping with the atmosphere of memory, the stage is dim. Shafts of light are focused on selected areas or actors, sometimes in contradistinction to what is the apparent centre. For instance, in the quarrel scene between TOM and AMANDA, in which LAURA has no active part, the clearest pool of light is on her figure. This is also true of the supper scene, when her silent figure on the sofa should remain the visual centre. The light upon LAURA should be distinct from the others, having a peculiar pristine clarity such as light used in early religious portraits of female saints or madonnas. A certain correspondence to light in religious paintings, such as El Greco's, where the figures are radiant in atmosphere that is relatively dusky, could be effectively used throughout the play. [It will also permit a more effective use of the screen.] A free, imaginative use of light can be of enormous value in giving a mobile, plastic quality to plays of a more or less static nature.   T.W.

Use audience + dramatic
Presentation

THE GLASS MENAGERIE

This play was first presented in London at the Theatre Royal, Haymarket, on 28 July 1948 with the following cast:

AMANDA WINGFIELD	*Helen Hayes*
LAURA, her daughter	*Frances Heflin*
TOM, her son	*Phil Brown*
THE GENTLEMAN CALLER	*Hugh McDermott*

The play directed by John Gielgud
Setting by Jo Mielziner. Original music composed
by Paul Bowles.
Dance music arranged by Leslie Bridgewater

Scene: An alley in St Louis
PART 1: Preparation for a Gentleman Caller
PART 2: The Gentleman Calls

Time: Now and the Past

talk - about characters + Tom

likeable, sympathetic, interesting, selfish & funny - how audience see these things

This is a play about a family + how their relationship is together - 1940 America

SCENE ONE

TOM doesn't think American society is good to be in !

The Wingfield apartment is in the rear of the building, one of those vast hive-like conglomerations of cellular living-units that flower as warty growths in overcrowded urban centres of lower-middle-class population and are symptomatic of the impulse of this largest and fundamentally enslaved section of American society to avoid fluidity and differentiation and to exist and function as one interfused mass of automatism.

The apartment faces an alley and is entered by a fire-escape, a structure whose name is a touch of accidental poetic truth, for all of these huge buildings are always burning with the slow and implacable fires of human desperation. The fire-escape is included in the set – that is, the landing of it and steps descending from it.

that's the way Tom sees it.

The scene is memory and is therefore non-realistic. Memory takes a lot of poetic licence. It omits some details; others are exaggerated, according to the emotional value of the articles it touches, for memory is seated predominantly in the heart. The interior is therefore rather dim and poetic.

[*At the rise of the curtain, the audience is faced with the dark, grim rear wall of the Wingfield tenement. This building, which runs parallel to the footlights, is flanked on both sides by dark, narrow alleys which run into murky canyons of tangled clothes-lines, garbage cans, and the sinister lattice-work of neighbouring fire-escapes. It is up and down these side alleys that exterior entrances and exits are made, during the play. At the end of* TOM'S *opening commentary, the dark tenement wall slowly reveals (by means of a transparency) the interior of the ground floor Wingfield apartment.*

Downstage is the living-room, which also serves as a sleeping-room for LAURA, *the sofa unfolding to make her bed. Upstage, centre, and divided by a wide arch or second proscenium with transparent faded portières (or second curtain), is*

play refers to great depression and economic problems faced in America

the dining-room. In an old-fashioned what-not in the living-room are seen scores of transparent glass animals. A blown-up photograph of the father hangs on the wall of the living-room, facing the audience, to the left of the archway. It is the face of a very handsome young man in a doughboy's First World War cap. He is gallantly smiling, ineluctably smiling, as if to say 'I will be smiling for ever'.

The audience hears and sees the opening scene in the dining-room through both the transparent fourth wall of the building and the transparent gauze portières of the dining-room arch. It is during this revealing scene that the fourth wall slowly ascends out of sight. This transparent exterior wall is not brought down again until the very end of the play, during TOM'S *final speech.*

The narrator is an undisguised convention of the play. He takes whatever licence with dramatic convention is convenient to his purposes.

TOM *enters dressed as a merchant sailor from alley, stage left, and strolls across the front of the stage to the fire-escape. There he stops and lights a cigarette. He addresses the audience.*]

TOM: Yes, I have tricks in my pocket, I have things up my sleeve. But I am the opposite of a stage magician. He gives you illusion that has the appearance of truth. I give you truth in the pleasant disguise of illusion.

To begin with, I turn back time. I reverse it to that quaint period, the thirties, when the huge middle class of America was matriculating in a school for the blind. Their eyes had failed them, or they had failed their eyes, and so they were having their fingers pressed forcibly down on the fiery Braille alphabet of a dissolving economy.

In Spain there was revolution. Here there was only shouting and confusion.

In Spain there was Guernica. Here there were disturbances of labour, sometimes pretty violent, in other-

wise peaceful cities such as Chicago, Cleveland, Saint
Louis. . . .
This is the social background of the play.

[MUSIC]

The play is memory.
Being a memory play, it is dimly lighted, it is sentimental,
it is not realistic.
In memory everything seems to happen to music. That
explains the fiddle in the wings.
I am the narrator of the play, and also a character in it.
The other characters are my mother Amanda, my sister
Laura, and a gentleman caller who appears in the final
scenes.
He is the most realistic character in the play, being an
emissary from a world of reality that we were somehow
set apart from.
But since I have a poet's weakness for symbols, I am
using this character also as a symbol; he is the long-
delayed but always expected something that we live for.
There is a fifth character in the play who doesn't appear
except in this larger-than-life-size photograph over the
mantel.
This is our father who left us a long time ago.
He was a telephone man who fell in love with long dis-
tances; he gave up his job with the telephone company
and skipped the light fantastic out of town. . . .
The last we heard of him was a picture postcard from
Mazatlan, on the Pacific coast of Mexico, containing a
message of two words –
'Hello – Good-bye!' and no address.
I think the rest of the play will explain itself. . . .

[AMANDA'S *voice becomes audible through the portières.*
LEGEND ON SCREEN: 'OÙ SONT LES NEIGES'.
He divides the portières and enters the upstage area.

AMANDA *and* LAURA *are seated at a drop-leaf table.*
Eating is indicated by gestures without food or utensils.
AMANDA *faces the audience.* TOM *and* LAURA *are seated*
in profile.

The interior has lit up softly and through the scrim we see
AMANDA *and* LAURA *seated at the table in the upstage*
area.]

AMANDA [*calling*]: Tom?

TOM: Yes, Mother.

AMANDA: We can't say grace until you come to the
table!

TOM: Coming, Mother. [*He bows slightly and withdraws, re-*
appearing a few moments later in his place at the table.]

AMANDA [*to her son*]: Honey, don't *push* with your *fingers*. If
you have to push with something, the thing to push with
is a crust of bread. And chew – chew! Animals have
sections in their stomachs which enable them to digest
food without mastication, but human beings are supposed to chew their food before they swallow it down.
Eat food leisurely, son, and really enjoy it. A well-cooked
meal has lots of delicate flavours that have to be held in
the mouth for appreciation. So chew your food and give
your salivary glands a chance to function!

[TOM *deliberately lays his imaginary fork down and pushes his*
chair back from the table.]

TOM: I haven't enjoyed one bite of this dinner because of
your constant directions on how to eat it. It's you that
makes me rush through meals with your hawk-like
attention to every bite I take. Sickening – spoils my
appetite – all this discussion of – animals' secretion –
salivary glands – mastication!

AMANDA [*lightly*]: Temperament like a Metropolitan star!
[*He rises and crosses downstage.*] You're not excused from
the table.

TOM: I'm getting a cigarette.

AMANDA: You smoke too much.

[LAURA *rises*.]

LAURA: I'll bring in the blancmange.

[*He remains standing with his cigarette by the portières during the following*.]

AMANDA [*rising*]: No, sister, no, sister – you be the lady this time and I'll be the darkey.

LAURA: I'm already up.

AMANDA: Resume your seat, little sister – I want you to stay fresh and pretty – for gentleman callers!

LAURA: I'm not expecting any gentleman callers.

AMANDA [*crossing out to kitchenette. Airily*]: Sometimes they come when they are least expected! Why, I remember one Sunday afternoon in Blue Mountain – [*Enters kitchenette*.]

TOM: I know what's coming!

LAURA: Yes. But let her tell it.

TOM: Again?

LAURA: She loves to tell it.

[AMANDA *returns with bowl of dessert*.]

AMANDA: One Sunday afternoon in Blue Mountain – your mother received – *seventeen!* – gentlemen callers! Why, sometimes there weren't chairs enough to accommodate them all. We had to send the nigger over to bring in folding chairs from the parish house.

TOM [*remaining at portières*]: How did you entertain those gentleman callers?

AMANDA: I understood the art of conversation!

TOM: I bet you could talk.

AMANDA: Girls in those days *knew* how to talk, I can tell you.

TOM: Yes?

[IMAGE: AMANDA AS A GIRL ON A PORCH, GREET-
ING CALLERS.]

AMANDA: They knew how to entertain their gentlemen
callers. It wasn't enough for a girl to be possessed of a
pretty face and a graceful figure – although I wasn't
slighted in either respect. She also needed to have a
nimble wit and a tongue to meet all occasions.

TOM: What did you talk about?

AMANDA: Things of importance going on in the world!
Never anything coarse or common or vulgar. [*She
addresses* TOM *as though he were seated in the vacant chair at the
table though he remains by portières. He plays this scene as
though he held the book.*] My callers were gentleman – all!
Among my callers were some of the most prominent
young planters of the Mississippi Delta – planters and
sons of planters!

[TOM *motions for music and a spot of light on* AMANDA.
*Her eyes lift, her face glows, her voice becomes rich and
elegiac.*
SCREEN LEGEND: 'OÙ SONT LES NEIGES'.]

There was young Champ Laughlin who later became
vice-president of the Delta Planters Bank.
Hadley Stevenson who was drowned in Moon Lake and
left his widow one hundred and fifty thousand in Govern-
ment bonds.
There were the Cutrere brothers, Wesley and Bates. Bates
was one of my bright particular beaux! He got in a
quarrel with that wild Wainwright boy. They shot it out
on the floor of Moon Lake Casino. Bates was shot through
the stomach. Died in the ambulance on his way to
Memphis. His widow was also well provided for, came
into eight or ten thousand acres, that's all. She married
him on the rebound – never loved her – carried my picture on him the night he died!

And there was that boy that every girl in the Delta had
set her cap for! That brilliant, brilliant young Fitzhugh
boy from Greene County!

TOM: What did he leave his widow?

AMANDA: He never married! Gracious, you talk as though
all of my old admirers had turned up their toes to the
daisies!

TOM: Isn't this the first you've mentioned that still survives?

AMANDA: That Fitzhugh boy went North and made a fortune – came to be known as the Wolf of Wall Street! He
had the Midas touch, whatever he touched turned to
gold!
And I could have been Mrs Duncan J. Fitzhugh, mind
you! But – I picked your *father*!

LAURA [*rising*]: Mother, let me clear the table.

AMANDA: No, dear, you go in front and study your type-
writer chart. Or practise your shorthand a little. Stay
fresh and pretty! – It's almost time for our gentlemen
callers to start arriving. [*She flounces girlishly toward the
kitchenette.*] How many do you suppose we're going to
entertain this afternoon?

[TOM *throws down the paper and jumps up with a groan.*]

LAURA [*alone in the dining-room*]: I don't believe we're going
to receive any, Mother.

AMANDA [*reappearing, airily*]: What? No one – not one?
You must be joking! [LAURA *nervously echoes her laugh.
She slips in a fugitive manner through the half-open portières and
draws them in gently behind her. A shaft of very clear light is
thrown on her face against the faded tapestry of the curtains.*]

[MUSIC: 'THE GLASS MENAGERIE' UNDER FAINTLY.
Lightly.]

Not one gentleman caller? It can't be true! There must
be a flood, there must have been a tornado!

LAURA: It isn't a flood, it's not a tornado, Mother. I'm just not popular like you were in Blue Mountain. ... [TOM *utters another groan.* LAURA *glances at him with a faint, apologetic smile. Her voice catching a little.*] Mother's afraid I'm going to be an old maid.

THE SCENE DIMS OUT WITH 'GLASS MENAGERIE' MUSIC

SCENE TWO

'Laura, Haven't you Ever Liked Some Boy?'
  On the dark stage the screen is lighted with the image of blue roses.

[*Gradually* LAURA'S *figure becomes apparent and the
screen goes out.*
  The music subsides.
  LAURA *is seated in the delicate ivory chair at the small
claw-foot table.*
  *She wears a dress of soft violet material for a kimono – her
hair tied back from her forehead with a ribbon.*
  She is washing and polishing her collection of glass.
  AMANDA *appears on the fire-escape steps. At the sound of
her ascent,* LAURA *catches her breath, thrusts the bowl of
ornaments away and seats herself stiffly before the diagram of
the typewriter keyboard as though it held her spellbound.*
  Something has happened to AMANDA. *It is written in her
face as she climbs to the landing: a look that is grim and hope-
less and a little absurd.*
  *She has on one of those cheap or imitation velvety-looking
cloth coats with imitation fur collar. Her hat is five or six years
old, one of those dreadful cloche hats that were worn in the late
twenties and she is clasping an enormous black patent-leather
pocketbook with nickel clasps and initials. This is her full-dress
outfit, the one she usually wears to the D.A.R.*
  Before entering she looks through the door.
  *She purses her lips, opens her eyes very wide, rolls them
upward, and shakes her head.*
  *Then she slowly lets herself in the door. Seeing her mother's
expression* LAURA *touches her lips with a nervous gesture.*]

LAURA: Hello, Mother, I was – [*She makes a nervous gesture
toward the chart on the wall.* AMANDA *leans against the shut
door and stares at* LAURA *with a martyred look.*]

AMANDA: Deception? Deception? [*She slowly removes her hat and gloves, continuing the sweet suffering stare. She lets the hat and gloves fall on the floor — a bit of acting.*]

LAURA [*shakily*]: How was the D.A.R. meeting? [AMANDA *slowly opens her purse and removes a dainty white handkerchief which she shakes out delicately and delicately touches to her lips and nostrils.*] Didn't you go to the D.A.R. meeting, Mother?

AMANDA [*faintly, almost inaudibly*]: – No. – No. [*Then more forcibly.*] I did not have the strength – to go to the D.A.R. In fact, I did not have the courage! I wanted to find a hole in the ground and hide myself in it for ever! [*She crosses slowly to the wall and removes the diagram of the type-writer keyboard. She holds it in front of her for a second, staring at it sweetly and sorrowfully — then bites her lips and tears it into two pieces.*]

LAURA [*faintly*]: Why did you do that, Mother? [AMANDA *repeats the same procedure with the chart of the Gregg alphabet.*] Why are you –?

AMANDA: Why? Why? How old are you, Laura?

LAURA: Mother, you know my age.

AMANDA: I thought that you were an adult; it seems that I was mistaken. [*She crosses slowly to the sofa and sinks down and stares at* LAURA.]

LAURA: Please don't stare at me, Mother.

[AMANDA *closes her eyes and lowers her head. Count ten.*]

AMANDA: What are we going to do, what is going to become of us, what is the future?

[*Count ten.*]

LAURA: Has something happened, Mother? [AMANDA *draws a long breath and takes out the handkerchief again. Dabbing process.*] Mother, has — something happened?

AMANDA: I'll be all right in a minute, I'm just bewildered — [*Count five.*] — by life. . . .

LAURA: Mother, I wish that you would tell me what's happened!

AMANDA: As you know, I was supposed to be inducted into my office at the D.A.R. this afternoon. [IMAGE: A SWARM OF TYPEWRITERS.] But I stopped off at Rubicam's business college to speak to your teachers about your having a cold and ask them what progress they thought you were making down there.

LAURA: Oh. . . .

AMANDA: I went to the typing instructor and introduced myself as your mother. She didn't know who you were. Wingfield, she said. We don't have any such student enrolled at the school!
I assured her she did, that you had been going to classes since early in January.
'I wonder,' she said, 'if you could be talking about that terribly shy little girl who dropped out of school after only a few days' attendance?'
'No,' I said, 'Laura, my daughter, has been going to school every day for the past six weeks!'
'Excuse me,' she said. She took the attendance book out and there was your name, unmistakably printed, and all the dates you were absent until they decided that you had dropped out of school.
I still said, 'No, there must have been some mistake! There must have been some mix-up in the records!'
And she said, 'No – I remember her perfectly now. Her hands shook so that she couldn't hit the right keys! The first time we gave a speed-test, she broke down completely – was sick at the stomach and almost had to be carried into the wash-room! After that morning she never showed up any more. We phoned the house but never got any answer' – while I was working at Famous and Barr, I suppose, demonstrating those – Oh!
I felt so weak I could barely keep on my feet!
I had to sit down while they got me a glass of water!

Fifty dollars' tuition, all of our plans – my hopes and
ambition for you – just gone up the spout, just gone up
the spout like that. [LAURA *draws a long breath and gets
awkwardly to her feet. She crosses to the victrola and winds it
up.*]
What are you doing?

LAURA: Oh! [*She releases the handle and returns to her seat.*]

AMANDA: Laura, where have you been going when you've
gone on pretending that you were going to business college?

LAURA: I've just been going out walking.

AMANDA: That's not true.

LAURA: It is. I just went walking.

AMANDA: Walking? Walking? In winter? Deliberately
courting pneumonia in that light coat? Where did you
walk to, Laura?

LAURA: All sorts of places – mostly in the park.

AMANDA: Even after you'd started catching that cold?

LAURA: It was the lesser of two evils, Mother. [IMAGE:
WINTER SCENE IN PARK.] I couldn't go back up. I –
threw up – on the floor!

AMANDA: From half past seven till after five every day you
mean to tell me you walked around in the park, because
you wanted to make me think that you were still going to
Rubicam's Business College?

LAURA: It wasn't as bad as it sounds. I went inside places to
get warmed up.

AMANDA: Inside where?

LAURA: I went in the art museum and the bird-houses at
the Zoo. I visited the penguins every day! Sometimes I
did without lunch and went to the movies. Lately I've
been spending most of my afternoons in the Jewel-box,
that big glass-house where they raise the tropical
flowers.

AMANDA: You did all this to deceive me, just for deception?
[LAURA *looks down.*] Why?

LAURA: Mother, when you're disappointed, you get that awful suffering look on your face, like the picture of Jesus' mother in the museum!

AMANDA: Hush!

LAURA: I couldn't face it.

[*Pause. A whisper of strings.*
    LEGEND: 'THE CRUST OF HUMILITY'.]

AMANDA [*hopelessly fingering the huge pocketbook*]: So what are we going to do the rest of our lives? Stay home and watch the parades go by? Amuse ourselves with the glass menagerie, darling? Eternally play those worn-out phonograph records your father left as a painful reminder of him? We won't have a business career – we've given that up because it gave us nervous indigestion! [*Laughs wearily.*] What is there left but dependency all our lives? I know so well what becomes of unmarried women who aren't prepared to occupy a position. I've seen such pitiful cases in the South – barely tolerated spinsters living upon the grudging patronage of sister's husband or brother's wife! – stuck away in some little mousetrap of a room – encouraged by one in-law to visit another – little birdlike women without any nest – eating the crust of humility all their life!

Is that the future that we've mapped out for ourselves? I swear it's the only alternative I can think of!

It isn't a very pleasant alternative, is it?

Of course – some girls *do marry.*

[LAURA *twists her hands nervously.*]

Haven't you ever liked some boy?

LAURA: Yes. I liked one once. [*Rises.*] I came across his picture a while ago.

AMANDA [*with some interest*]: He gave you his picture?

LAURA: No, it's in the year-book.

AMANDA: [*disappointed*]: Oh – a high-school boy.

[SCREEN IMAGE: JIM AS HIGH-SCHOOL HERO BEAR-
ING A SILVER CUP.]

LAURA: Yes. His name was Jim. [LAURA *lifts the heavy annual from the claw-foot table.*] Here he is in *The Pirates of Penzance.*

AMANDA [*absently*]: The what?

LAURA: The operetta the senior class put on. He had a won-derful voice and we sat across the aisle from each other Mondays, Wednesdays, and Fridays in the Aud. Here he is with the silver cup for debating! See his grin?

AMANDA [*absently*]: He must have had a jolly disposition.

LAURA: He used to call me – Blue Roses.

[IMAGE: BLUE ROSES.]

AMANDA: Why did he call you such a name as that?

LAURA: When I had that attack of pleurosis – he asked me what was the matter when I came back. I said pleurosis – he thought that I said Blue Roses! So that's what he always called me after that. Whenever he saw me, he'd holler, 'Hello, Blue Roses!' I didn't care for the girl that he went out with. Emily Meisenbach. Emily was the best-dressed girl at Soldan. She never struck me, though, as being sincere. . . . It says in the Personal Section – they're engaged. That's – six years ago! They must be married by now.

AMANDA: Girls that aren't cut out for business careers usually wind up married to some nice man. [*Gets up with a spark of revival.*] Sister, that's what you'll do!

[LAURA *utters a startled, doubtful laugh. She reaches quickly for a piece of glass.*]

LAURA: But, Mother –

AMANDA: Yes? [*Crossing to photograph.*]

LAURA [*in a tone of frightened apology*]: I'm – crippled!

[IMAGE: SCREEN.]

AMANDA: Nonsense! Laura, I've told you never, never to use that word. Why, you're not crippled, you just have a little defect – hardly noticeable, even! When people have some slight disadvantage like that, they cultivate other things to make up for it – develop charm – and vivacity – and – *charm!* That's all you have to do! [*She turns again to the photograph.*] One thing your father had *plenty of* – was *charm!*

[TOM *motions to the fiddle in the wings.*]

THE SCENE FADES OUT WITH MUSIC

SCENE THREE

LEGEND ON SCREEN: 'AFTER THE FIASCO –'

[TOM *speaks from the fire-escape landing.*]

TOM: After the fiasco at Rubicam's Business College, the idea of getting a gentleman caller for Laura began to play a more and more important part in Mother's calculations. It became an obsession. Like some archetype of the universal unconscious, the image of the gentleman caller haunted our small apartment. . . .

[IMAGE: YOUNG MAN AT DOOR WITH FLOWERS.]

An evening at home rarely passed without some allusion to this image, this spectre, this hope. . . .
Even when he wasn't mentioned, his presence hung in Mother's preoccupied look and in my sister's frightened, apologetic manner – hung like a sentence passed upon the Wingfields!
Mother was a woman of action as well as words.
She began to take logical steps in the planned direction.
Late that winter and in the early spring – realizing that extra money would be needed to properly feather the nest and plume the bird – she conducted a vigorous campaign on the telephone, roping in subscribers to one of those magazines for matrons called *The Home-maker's Companion*, the type of journal that features the serialized sublimations of ladies of letters who think in terms of delicate cup-like breasts, slim, tapering waists, rich, creamy thighs, eyes like wood-smoke in autumn, fingers that soothe and caress like strains of music, bodies as powerful as Etruscan sculpture.

[SCREEN IMAGE: GLAMOUR MAGAZINE COVER.]

[AMANDA *enters with phone on long extension cord. She is spotted in the dim stage.*]

AMANDA: Ida Scott? This is Amanda Wingfield!
We *missed* you at the D.A.R. last Monday!
I said to myself: She's probably suffering with that sinus condition! How is that sinus condition?
Horrors! Heaven have mercy! – You're a Christian martyr, yes, that's what you are, a Christian martyr!
Well, I just have happened to notice that your subscription to the *Companion*'s about to expire! Yes, it expires with the next issue, honey! – just when that wonderful new serial by Bessie Mae Hopper is getting off to such an exciting start. Oh, honey, it's something that you can't miss! You remember how *Gone With the Wind* took everybody by storm? You simply couldn't go out if you hadn't read it. All everybody *talked* was Scarlet O'Hara. Well, this is a book that critics already compare to *Gone With the Wind*. It's the *Gone With the Wind* of the post-World War generation! – What? – Burning! – Oh, honey, don't let them burn, go take a look in the oven and I'll hold the wire! Heavens – I think she's hung up!

[DIM OUT]

[LEGEND ON SCREEN: 'YOU THINK I'M IN LOVE WITH CONTINENTAL SHOEMAKERS?']

[*Before the stage is lighted, the violent voices of* TOM *and* AMANDA *are heard.*
The are quarrelling behind the portières. In front of them stands LAURA *with clenched hands and panicky expression.*
A clear pool of light on her figure throughout this scene.]

TOM: What in Christ's name am I –
AMANDA [*shrilly*]: Don't you use that –
TOM: Supposed to do!
AMANDA: Expression! Not in my –

TOM: Ohhh!

AMANDA: Presence! Have you gone out of your senses?

TOM: I have, that's true, *driven* out!

AMANDA: What is the matter with you, you – big – big IDIOT!

TOM: Look! – I've got *no thing*, no single thing –

AMANDA: Lower your voice!

TOM: In my life here that I can call my OWN! Everything is –

AMANDA: Stop that shouting!

TOM: Yesterday you confiscated my books! You had the nerve to –

AMANDA: I took that horrible novel back to the library – yes! That hideous book by that insane Mr Lawrence. [TOM *laughs wildly.*] I cannot control the output of diseased minds or people who cater to them – [TOM *laughs still more wildly.*] BUT I WON'T ALLOW SUCH FILTH BROUGHT INTO MY HOUSE! No, no, no, no, no!

TOM: House, house! Who pays rent on it, who makes a slave of himself to –

AMANDA [*fairly screeching*]: Don't you DARE to –

TOM: No, no, *I* mustn't say things! *I've* got to just –

AMANDA: Let me tell you –

TOM: I don't want to hear any more! [*He tears the portières open. The upstage area is lit with a turgid smoky red glow.*]

[AMANDA'S *hair is in metal curlers and she wears a very old bathrobe, much too large for her slight figure, a relic of the faithless Mr Wingfield. An upright typewriter and a wild disarray of manuscripts are on the drop-leaf table. The quarrel was probably precipitated by* AMANDA'S *interruption of his creative labour. A chair lying overthrown on the floor.*

Their gesticulating shadows are cast on the ceiling by the fiery glow.]

AMANDA: You *will* hear more, you –

TOM: No, I won't hear more, I'm going out!

AMANDA: You come right back in –

TOM: Out, out, out! Because I'm –

AMANDA: Come back here, Tom Wingfield! I'm not through talking to you!

TOM: Oh, go –

LAURA [*desperately*]: – Tom!

AMANDA: You're going to listen, and no more insolence from you! I'm at the end of my patience!

[*He comes back toward her.*]

TOM: What do you think I'm at? Aren't I supposed to have any patience to reach the end of, Mother? I know, I know. It seems unimportant to you, what I'm *doing* – what I *want* to do – having a little *difference* between them! You don't think that –

AMANDA: I think you've been doing things that you're ashamed of. That's why you act like this. I don't believe that you go every night to the movies. Nobody goes to the movies night after night. Nobody in their right mind goes to the movies as often as you pretend to. People don't go to the movies at nearly midnight, and movies don't let out at two a.m. Come in stumbling. Muttering to yourself like a maniac! You get three hours' sleep and then go to work. Oh, I can picture the way you're doing down there. Moping, doping, because you're in no condition.

TOM [*wildly*]: No, I'm in no condition!

AMANDA: What right have you got to jeopardize your job? Jeopardize the security of us all? How do you think we'd manage if you were –

TOM: Listen! You think I'm crazy about the *warehouse*? [*He bends fiercely toward her slight figure.*] You think I'm in love with the Continental Shoemakers? You think I want to spend fifty-five *years* down there in that – *celotex interior*! with – *fluorescent* – *tubes*! Look! I'd rather somebody picked up a crowbar and battered out my brains – than go back mornings! I *go*! Every time you come in yelling

that God damn '*Rise and Shine!*' '*Rise and Shine!*' I say to
myself, 'How lucky dead people are!' But I get up. I *go!* For
sixty-five dollars a month I give up all that I dream
of doing and being *ever!* And you say self – self's' all I
ever think of. Why, listen, if self is what I thought of,
Mother, I'd be where he is – GONE! [*Pointing to father's
picture.*] As far as the system of transportation reaches!
[*He starts past her. She grabs his arm.*] Don't grab at me,
Mother!

AMANDA: Where are you going?

TOM: I'm going to the *movies!*

AMANDA: I don't believe that lie!

TOM [*crouching toward her, overtowering her tiny figure. She backs
away, gasping*]: I'm going to opium dens! Yes, opium
dens, dens of vice and criminals' hang-outs, Mother. I've
joined the Hogan gang, I'm a hired assassin, I carry a
tommy-gun in a violin case! I run a string of cat-houses
in the Valley! They call me Killer, Killer Wingfield, I'm
leading a double-life, a simple, honest warehouse worker
by day, by night a dynamic *tsar* of the *underworld, Mother*.
I go to gambling casinos, I spin away fortunes on the
roulette table! I wear a patch over one eye and a false
moustache, sometimes I put on green whiskers. On those
occasions they call me – *El Diablo!* Oh, I could tell you
things to make you sleepless! My enemies plan to dyna-
mite this place. They're going to blow us all sky-high
some night! I'll be glad, very happy, and so will you!
You'll go up, up on a broomstick, over Blue Mountain
with seventeen gentlemen callers! You ugly – babbling
old – witch. ... [*He goes through a series of violent, clumsy
movements, seizing his overcoat, lunging to the door, pulling it
fiercely open. The women watch him, aghast. His arm catches in
the sleeve of the coat as he struggles to pull it on. For a moment
he is pinioned by the bulky garment. With an outraged groan he
tears the coat off again, splitting the shoulder of it, and hurls it
across the room. It strikes against the shelf of* LAURA'S *glass*

collection, there is a tinkle of shattering glass. LAURA *cries out as if wounded.*]

[MUSIC. LEGEND: 'THE GLASS MENAGERIE'.]

LAURA [*shrilly*]: *My glass!* – menagerie. .... [*She covers her face and turns away.*]

[*But* AMANDA *is still stunned and stupefied by the 'ugly witch' so that she barely notices this occurrence. Now she recovers her speech.*]

AMANDA [*in an awful voice*]: I won't speak to you – until you apologize! [*She crosses through portières and draws them together behind her.* TOM *is left with* LAURA. LAURA *clings weakly to the mantel with her face averted.* TOM *stares at her stupidly for a moment. Then he crosses to shelf. Drops awkwardly on his knees to collect the fallen glass, glancing at* LAURA *as if he would speak but couldn't.*]

'*The Glass Menagerie*' *steals in as*

THE SCENE DIMS OUT

SCENE FOUR

The interior is dark. Faint light in the alley.

A deep-voiced bell in a church is tolling the hour of five as the scene commences.

[TOM *appears at the top of the alley. After each solemn boom of the bell in the tower, he shakes a little noise-maker or rattle as if to express the tiny spasm of man in contrast to the sustained power and dignity of the Almighty. This and the unsteadiness of his advance make it evident that he has been drinking.*

As he climbs the few steps to the fire-escape landing light steals up inside. LAURA *appears in night-dress, observing* TOM'S *empty bed in the front room.*

TOM *fishes in his pockets for door-key, removing a motley assortment of articles in the search, including a perfect shower of movie-ticket stubs and an empty bottle. At last he finds the key, but just as he is about to insert it, it slips from his fingers. He strikes a match and crouches below the door.*]

TOM [*bitterly*]: One crack – and it falls through!

[LAURA *opens the door.*]

LAURA: Tom! Tom, what are you doing?
TOM: Looking for a door-key.
LAURA: Where have you been all this time?
TOM: I have been to the movies.
LAURA: All this time at the movies?
TOM: There was a very long programme. There was a Garbo picture and a Mickey Mouse and a travelogue and a newsreel and a preview of coming attractions. And there was an organ solo and a collection for the milk-fund – simultaneously – which ended up in a terrible fight between a fat lady and an usher!

LAURA [*innocently*]: Did you have to stay through everything?

TOM: Of course! And, oh, I forgot! There was a big stage show! The headliner on this stage show was Malvolio the Magician. He performed wonderful tricks, many of them, such as pouring water back and forth between pitchers. First it turned to wine and then it turned to beer and then it turned to whisky. I knew it was whisky it finally turned into because he needed somebody to come up out of the audience to help him, and I came up – both shows! It was Kentucky Straight Bourbon. A very generous fellow, he gave souvenirs. [*He pulls from his back pocket a shimmering rainbow-coloured scarf.*] He gave me this. This is his magic scarf. You can have it, Laura. You wave it over a canary cage and you get a bowl of gold-fish. You wave it over the gold-fish bowl and they fly away canaries. . . . But the wonderfullest trick of all was the coffin trick. We nailed him into a coffin and he got out of the coffin without removing one nail. [*He has come inside.*] There is a trick that would come in handy for me – get me out of this 2 by 4 situation! [*Flops on to a bed and starts removing shoes.*]

LAURA: Tom – Shhh'!

TOM: What're you shushing me for?

LAURA: You'll wake up mother.

TOM: Goody, goody! Pay 'er back for all those 'Rise an' Shines'. [*Lies down, groaning.*] You know it don't take much intelligence to get yourself into a nailed-up coffin, Laura. But who in hell ever got himself out of one without removing one nail?

[*As if in answer, the father's grinning photograph lights up.*]

[SCENE DIMS OUT.]

[*Immediately following: The church bell is heard striking six. At the sixth stroke the alarm clock goes off in* AMANDA'S *room, and after a few moments we hear her calling 'Rise and:*

*Shine! Rise and Shine! Laura, go tell your brother to rise and
shine!'*]

TOM [*sitting up slowly*]: I'll rise – but I won't shine.

[*The light increases.*]

AMANDA: Laura, tell your brother his coffee is ready.

[LAURA *slips into front room.*]

LAURA: Tom! – It's nearly seven. Don't make mother nervous. [*He stares at her stupidly. Beseechingly.*] Tom, speak to
mother this morning. Make up with her, apologize, speak
to her!

TOM: She won't to me. It's her that started not speaking.

LAURA: If you just say you're sorry she'll start speaking.

TOM: Her not speaking – is that such a tragedy?

LAURA: Please – please!

AMANDA [*calling from kitchenette*]: Laura, are you going to do
what I asked you to do, or do I have to get dressed and go
out myself?

LAURA: Going, going – soon as I get on my coat! [*She pulls
on a shapeless felt hat with nervous, jerky movement, pleadingly
glancing at* TOM. *Rushes awkwardly for coat. The coat is one of*
AMANDA'S, *inaccurately made-over, the sleeves too short for*
LAURA.] Butter and what else?

AMANDA [*entering upstage*]: Just butter. Tell them to charge
it.

LAURA: Mother, they make such faces when I do that.

AMANDA: Sticks and stones can break our bones, but the
expression on Mr Garfinkel's face won't harm us! Tell
your brother his coffee is getting cold.

LAURA [*at door*]: Do what I asked you, will you, will you,
Tom?

[*He looks sullenly away.*]

AMANDA: Laura, go now or just don't go at all!

LAURA [*rushing out*]: Going – going ! [*A second later she cries out.* TOM *springs up and crosses to door.* AMANDA *rushes anxiously in.* TOM *opens the door.*]

TOM: Laura?

LAURA: I'm all right. I slipped, but I'm all right.

AMANDA [*peering anxiously after her*]: If anyone breaks a leg on those fire-escape steps, the landlord ought to be sued for every cent he possesses ! [*She shuts door. Remembers she isn't speaking and returns to other room.*]

[*As* TOM *enters listlessly for his coffee, she turns her back to him and stands rigidly facing the window on the gloomy grey vault of the areaway. Its light on her face with its aged but childish features is cruelly sharp, satirical as a Daumier print.*

MUSIC UNDER: 'AVE MARIA'.

TOM *glances sheepishly but sullenly at her averted figure and slumps at the table. The coffee is scalding hot; he sips it and gasps and spits it back in the cup. At his gasp,* AMANDA *catches her breath and half turns. Then catches herself and turns back to window.*

TOM *blows on his coffee, glancing sidewise at his mother. She clears her throat.* TOM *clears his. He starts to rise. Sinks back down again, scratches his head, clears his throat again.* AMANDA *coughs.* TOM *raises his cup in both hands to blow on it, his eyes staring over the rim of it at his mother for several moments. Then he slowly sets the cup down and awkwardly and hesitantly rises from the chair.*]

TOM [*hoarsely*]: Mother. I – I apologize, Mother. [AMANDA *draws a quick, shuddering breath. Her face works grotesquely. She breaks into childlike tears.*] I'm sorry for what I said, for everything that I said; I didn't mean it.

AMANDA [*sobbingly*]: My devotion has made me a witch and so I make myself hateful to my children !

TOM: *No*, you *don't*.

AMANDA: I worry so much, don't sleep, it makes me nervous !

TOM [*gently*]: I understand that.

AMANDA: I've had to put up a solitary battle all these years. But you're my right-hand bower ! Don't fall down, don't fail !

TOM [*gently*]: I try, Mother.

AMANDA [*with great enthusiasm*]: Try and you will SUCCEED ! [*The notion makes her breathless.*] Why, you – you're just *full* of natural endowments ! Both of my children – they're *unusual* children ! Don't you think I know it? I'm so – *proud!* Happy and – feel I've – so much to be thankful for but – Promise me one thing, Son !

TOM: What, Mother?

AMANDA: Promise, Son, you'll – never be a drunkard !

TOM [*turns to her grinning*]: I will never be a drunkard, Mother.

AMANDA: That's what frightened me so, that you'd be drinking ! Eat a bowl of Purina !

TOM: Just coffee, Mother.

AMANDA: Shredded wheat biscuit?

TOM: No. No, Mother, just coffee.

AMANDA: You can't put in a day's work on an empty stomach. You've got ten minutes – don't gulp ! Drinking too-hot liquids makes cancer of the stomach. ... Put cream in.

TOM: No, thank you.

AMANDA: To cool it.

TOM: No ! No, thank you, I want it black.

AMANDA: I know, but it's not good for you. We have to do all that we can to build ourselves up. In these trying times we live in, all that we have to cling to is – each other. ... That's why it's so important to – Tom, I – I sent out your sister so I could discuss something with you. If you hadn't spoken I would have spoken to you. [*Sits down.*]

TOM [*gently*]: What is it, Mother, that you want to discuss?

AMANDA: *Laura!*

[TOM *puts his cup down slowly.*

LEGEND ON SCREEN: 'LAURA'.
MUSIC: 'THE GLASS MENAGERIE'.]

TOM: – Oh. – Laura . . .

AMANDA [*touching his sleeve*]: You know how, Laura is. So quiet but – still water runs deep ! She notices things and I think she – broods about them. [TOM *looks up.*] A few days ago I came in and she was crying.

TOM: What about?

AMANDA: You.

TOM: Me?

AMANDA: She has an idea that you're not happy here.

TOM: What gave her that idea?

AMANDA: What gives her any idea? However, you do act strangely. I – I'm not criticizing, understand *that* ! I know your ambitions do not lie in the warehouse, that like everybody in the whole wide world – you've had to – make sacrifices, but – Tom – Tom – life's not easy, it calls for – Spartan endurance ! There's so many things in my heart that I cannot describe to you ! I've never told you but I – *loved* your father. . . .

TOM [*gently*]: I know that, Mother.

AMANDA: And you – when I see you taking after his ways ! Staying out late – and – well, you *had* been drinking the night you were in that – terrifying condition ! Laura says that you hate the apartment and that you go out nights to get away from it ! Is that true, Tom?

TOM: No. You say there's so much in your heart that you can't describe to me. That's true of me, too. There's so much in my heart that I can't describe to *you* ! So let's respect each other's –

AMANDA: But, why – *why*, Tom – are you always so *restless*? Where do you *go* to, nights?

TOM: I – go to the movies.

AMANDA: Why do you go to the movies so much, Tom?

TOM: I go to the movies because – I like adventure.

Adventure is something I don't have much of at work, so I go to the movies. — Hates work

AMANDA: But, Tom, you go to the movies *entirely* too *much*!

TOM: I like a lot of adventure.

[AMANDA *looks baffled, then hurt. As the familiar inquisition resumes he becomes hard and impatient again.* AMANDA *slips back into her querulous attitude towards him.*

IMAGE ON SCREEN: SAILING VESSEL WITH JOLLY ROGER.]

AMANDA: Most young men find adventure in their careers.

TOM: Then most young men are not employed in a warehouse.

AMANDA: The world is full of young men employed in warehouses and offices and factories.

TOM: Do all of them find adventure in their careers?

AMANDA: They do or they do without it! Not everybody has a craze for adventure.

TOM: Man is by instinct a lover, a hunter, a fighter, and none of those instincts are given much play at the warehouse!

AMANDA: Man is by instinct! Don't quote instinct to me! Instinct is something that people have got away from! It belongs to animals! Christian adults don't want it!

TOM: What do Christian adults want, then, Mother?

AMANDA: Superior things! Things of the mind and the spirit! Only animals have to satisfy instincts! Surely your aims are somewhat higher than theirs! Than monkeys — pigs —

TOM: I reckon they're not.

AMANDA: You're joking. However, that isn't what I wanted to discuss.

TOM [*rising*]: I haven't much time.

AMANDA [*pushing his shoulders*]: Sit down.

TOM: You want me to punch in red at the warehouse, Mother?

AMANDA: You have five minutes. I want to talk about Laura.

[LEGEND: 'PLANS AND PROVISIONS'.]

TOM: All right! What about Laura?

AMANDA: We have to be making some plans and provisions for her. She's older than you, two years, and nothing has happened. She just drifts along doing nothing. It frightens me terribly how she just drifts along.

TOM: I guess she's the type that people call home girls.

AMANDA: There's no such type, and if there is, it's a pity! That is unless the home is hers, with a husband!

TOM: What?

AMANDA: Oh, I can see the handwriting on the wall as plain as I see the nose in front of my face! It's terrifying! More and more you remind me of your father! He was out all hours without explanation! – Then *left*! *Good-bye*! And me with the bag to hold. I saw that letter you got from the Merchant Marine. I know what you're dreaming of. I'm not standing here blindfolded.

Very well, then. Then *do* it!

But not till there's somebody to take your place.

TOM: What do you mean?

AMANDA: I mean that as soon as Laura has got somebody to take care of her, married, a home of her own, independent – why, then you'll be free to go wherever you please, on land, on sea, whichever way the wind blows you!

But until that time you've got to look out for your sister. I don't say me because I'm old and don't matter! I say for your sister because she's young and dependent.

I put her in business college – a dismal failure! Frightened her so it made her sick at the stomach.

I took her over to the Young People's League at the church. Another fiasco. She spoke to nobody, nobody spoke to her. Now all she does is fool with those pieces

of glass and play those worn-out records. What kind of a
life is that for a girl to lead?

TOM: What can I do about it?

AMANDA: Overcome selfishness!
Self, self, self is all that you ever think of!

[TOM *springs up and crosses to get his coat. It is ugly and
bulky. He pulls on a cap with earmuffs.*]

Where is your muffler? Put your wool muffler on! [*He
snatches it angrily from the closet and tosses it around his neck and
pulls both ends tight.*] Tom! I haven't said what I had in
mind to ask you.

TOM: I'm too late to –

AMANDA [*catching his arm – very importunately. Then shyly*]:
Down at the warehouse, aren't there some – nice young
men?

TOM: No!

AMANDA: There *must* be – *some* . . .

TOM: Mother –

[*Gesture.*]

AMANDA: Find out one that's clean-living – doesn't drink
and – ask him out for sister!

TOM: What?

AMANDA: For *sister*! To *meet*! Get *acquainted*!

TOM [*stamping to door*]: Oh, my go-osh!

AMANDA: Will you? [*He opens door. Imploringly.*] Will you?
[*He starts down.*] Will you? *Will* you, dear?

TOM [*calling back*]: YES!

[AMANDA *closes the door hesitantly and with a troubled but
faintly hopeful expression.*
SCREEN IMAGE: GLAMOUR MAGAZINE COVER.
Spot AMANDA *at phone.*]

AMANDA: Ella Cartwright? This is Amanda Wingfield!
How are you, honey?

How is that kidney condition?

[*Count five.*]

Horrors!

[*Count five.*]

You're a Christian martyr, yes, honey, that's what you are, a Christian martyr!

Well, I just now happened to notice in my little red book that your subscription to the *Companion* has just run out! I knew that you wouldn't want to miss out on the wonderful serial starting in this issue. It's by Bessie Mae Hopper, the first thing she's written since *Honeymoon for Three.*

Wasn't that a strange and interesting story? Well, this one is even lovelier, I believe. It has a sophisticated, society background. It's all about the horsy set on Long Island!

FADE OUT

Amanda sells love magazines for a living

SCENE FIVE *announcement*

LEGEND ON SCREEN: 'ANNUNCIATION'. *Fade with music.*
[*It is early dusk on a spring evening. Supper has just been finished in the Wingfield apartment.* AMANDA *and* LAURA *in light-coloured dresses are removing dishes from the table, in the upstage area, which is shadowy, their movements formalized almost as a dance or ritual, their moving forms as pale and silent as moths.*

TOM, *in white shirt and trousers, rises from the table and crosses toward the fire-escape.*]

AMANDA [*as he passes her*]: Son, will you do me a favour?

TOM: What?

AMANDA: Comb your hair! You look so pretty when your hair is combed! [TOM *slouches on sofa with evening paper. Enormous caption 'Franco Triumphs'.*] There is only one respect in which I would like you to emulate your father.

TOM: What respect is that?

AMANDA: The care he always took of his appearance. He never allowed himself to look untidy. [*He throws down the paper and crosses to fire-escape.*] Where are you going?

TOM: I'm going out to smoke.

AMANDA: You smoke too much. A pack a day at fifteen cents a pack. How much would that amount to in a month? Thirty times fifteen is how much, Tom? Figure it out and you will be astounded at what you could save. Enough to give you a night-school course in accounting at Washington U! Just think what a wonderful thing that would be for you, Son!

[TOM *is unmoved by the thought.*]

TOM: I'd rather smoke. [*He steps out on the landing, letting the screen door slam.*]

AMANDA [*sharply*]: I know! That's the tragedy of it. . . .
[*Alone, she turns to look at her husband's picture.*]

[DANCE MUSIC: 'ALL THE WORLD IS WAITING FOR
THE SUNRISE!']

TOM [*to the audience*]: Across the alley from us was the Paradise Dance Hall. On evenings in spring the windows and
doors were open and the music came outdoors. Sometimes
the lights were turned out except for a large glass sphere
that hung from the ceiling. It would turn slowly about
and filter the dusk with delicate rainbow colours. Then
the orchestra played a waltz or a tango, something that
had a slow and sensuous rhythm. Couples would come
outside, to the relative privacy of the alley. You could see
them kissing behind ash-pits and telegraph poles.
This was the compensation for lives that passed like mine,
without any change or adventure.
Adventure and change were imminent in this year. They
were waiting around the corner for all these kids.
Suspended in the mist over Berchtesgaden, caught in the
folds of Chamberlain's umbrella –
In Spain there was Guernica!
But here there was only hot swing music and liquor,
dance halls, bars, and movies, and sex that hung in the
gloom like a chandelier and flooded the world with brief,
deceptive rainbows. . . .
All the world was waiting for bombardments!

[AMANDA *turns from the picture and comes outside.*]

AMANDA [*sighing*]: A fire-escape landing's a poor excuse for
a porch. [*She spreads a newspaper on a step and sits down grace-
fully and demurely as if she were settling into a swing on a
Mississippi veranda.*] What are you looking at?
TOM: The moon.
AMANDA: Is there a moon this evening?
TOM: It's rising over Garfinkel's Delicatessen.

AMANDA: So it is ! A little silver slipper of a moon. Have you made a wish on it yet?

TOM: Um-hum.

AMANDA: What did you wish for?

TOM: That's a secret.

AMANDA: A secret, huh? Well, I won't tell mine either. I will be just as mysterious as you.

TOM: I bet I can guess what yours is.

AMANDA: Is my head so transparent?

TOM: You're not a sphinx.

AMANDA: No, I don't have secrets. I'll tell you what I wished for on the moon. Success and happiness for my precious children ! I wish for that whenever there's a moon, and when there isn't a moon, I wish for it, too.

TOM: I thought perhaps you wished for a gentleman caller.

AMANDA: Why do you say that?

TOM: Don't you remember asking me to fetch one?

AMANDA: I remember suggesting that it would be nice for your sister if you brought home some nice young man from the warehouse. I think that I've made that suggestion more than once.

TOM: Yes, you have made it repeatedly.

AMANDA: Well?

TOM: We are going to have one.

AMANDA: *What?*

TOM: A gentleman caller !

> [THE ANNUNCIATION IS CELEBRATED WITH MUSIC.
> AMANDA *rises.*
>
>   IMAGE ON SCREEN: CALLER WITH BOUQUET.]

AMANDA: You mean you have asked some nice young man to come over?

TOM: Yep. I've asked him to dinner.

AMANDA: You really did?

TOM: I did !

AMANDA: You did, and did he – *accept?*

TOM: He did!

AMANDA: Well, well – well, well! That's – lovely!

TOM: I thought that you would be pleased.

AMANDA: It's definite, then?

TOM: Very definite.

AMANDA: Soon?

TOM: Very soon.

AMANDA: For heaven's sake, stop putting on and tell me some things, will you?

TOM: What things do you want me to tell you?

AMANDA: *Naturally* I would like to know when he's *coming!*

TOM: He's coming tomorrow.

AMANDA: *Tomorrow?*

TOM: Yep. Tomorrow.

AMANDA: But, Tom!

TOM: Yes, Mother?

AMANDA: Tomorrow gives me no time!

TOM: Time for what?

AMANDA: Preparations! Why didn't you phone me at once, as soon as you asked him, the minute that he accepted? Then, don't you see, I could have been getting ready!

TOM: You don't have to make any fuss.

AMANDA: Oh, Tom, Tom, Tom, of course I have to make a fuss! I want things nice, not sloppy! Not thrown together. I'll certainly have to do some fast thinking, won't I?

TOM: I don't see why you have to think at all.

AMANDA: You just don't know. We can't have a gentleman caller in a pigsty! All my wedding silver has to be polished, the monogrammed table linen ought to be laundered! The windows have to be washed and fresh curtains put up. And how about clothes? We have to *wear* something, don't we?

TOM: Mother, this boy is no one to make a fuss over!

AMANDA: Do you realize he's the first young man we've introduced to your sister?

It's terrible, dreadful, disgraceful that poor little sister has never received a single gentleman caller! Tom, come inside! [*She opens the screen door.*]

TOM: What for?

AMANDA: I want to ask you some things.

TOM: If you're going to make such a fuss, I'll call it off, I'll tell him not to come!

AMANDA: You certainly won't do anything of the kind. Nothing offends people worse than broken engagements. It simply means I'll have to work like a Turk! We won't be brilliant, but we will pass inspection. Come on inside. [TOM *follows, groaning.*] Sit down.

TOM: Any particular place you would like me to sit?

AMANDA: Thank heavens I've got that new sofa! I'm also making payments on a floor lamp I'll have sent out! And put the chintz covers on, they'll brighten things up! Of course I'd hoped to have these walls re-papered. ... What is the young man's name?

TOM: His name is O'Connor.

AMANDA: That, of course, means fish – tomorrow is Friday! I'll have that salmon loaf – with Durkee's dressing! What does he do? He works at the warehouse?

TOM: Of course! How else would I –

AMANDA: Tom, he – doesn't drink?

TOM: Why do you ask me that?

AMANDA: Your father *did!*

TOM: Don't get started on that!

AMANDA: He *does* drink, then?

TOM: Not that I know of!

AMANDA: Make sure, be certain! The last thing I want for my daughter's a boy who drinks!

TOM: Aren't you being a little bit premature? Mr O'Connor has not yet appeared on the scene!

AMANDA: But will tomorrow. To meet your sister, and what do I know about his character? Nothing! Old maids are better off than wives of drunkards!

TOM: Oh, my God!

AMANDA: Be still!

TOM [*leaning forward to whisper*]: Lots of fellows meet girls whom they don't marry!

AMANDA: Oh, talk sensibly, Tom – and don't be sarcastic!

[*She has gotten a hairbrush.*]

TOM: What are you doing?

AMANDA: I'm brushing that cow-lick down!
What is this young man's position at the warehouse?

TOM [*submitting grimly to the brush and the interrogation*]: This young man's position is that of a shipping clerk, Mother.

AMANDA: Sounds to me like a fairly responsible job, the sort of a job *you* would be in if you just had more *get-up*.
What is his salary? Have you any idea?

TOM: I would judge it to be approximately eighty-five dollars a month.

AMANDA: Well – not princely, but –

TOM: Twenty more than I make.

AMANDA: Yes, how well I know! But for a family man, eighty-five dollars a month is not much more than you can just get by on. ...

TOM: Yes, but Mr O'Connor is not a family man.

AMANDA: He might be, mightn't he? Some time in the future?

TOM: I see. Plans and provisions.

AMANDA: You are the only young man that I know of who ignores the fact that the future becomes the present, the present the past, and the past turns into everlasting regret if you don't plan for it!

TOM: I will think that over and see what I can make of it.

AMANDA: Don't be supercilious with your mother! Tell me some more about this – what do you call him?

TOM: James D. O'Connor. The D. is for Delaney.

AMANDA: Irish on *both* sides! *Gracious!* And doesn't drink?

TOM: Shall I call him up and ask him right this minute?

AMANDA: The only way to find out about those things is
to make discreet inquiries at the proper moment. When I
was a girl in Blue Mountain and it was suspected that a
young man drank, the girl whose attentions he had been
receiving, if any girl *was*, would sometimes speak to the
minister of his church, or rather her father would if her
father was living, and sort of feel him out on the young
man's character. That is the way such things are discreetly handled to keep a young woman from making a
tragic mistake!

TOM: Then how did you happen to make a tragic mistake!

AMANDA: That innocent look of your father's had everyone fooled! He *smiled* – the world was *enchanted*!
No girl can do worse than put herself at the mercy of a
handsome appearance!
I hope that Mr O'Connor is not too good-looking.

TOM: No, he's not too good-looking. He's covered with
freckles and hasn't too much of a nose.

AMANDA: He's not right-down homely, though?

TOM: Not right-down homely. Just medium homely, I'd say.

AMANDA: Character's what to look for in a man.

TOM: That's what I've always said, Mother.

AMANDA: You've never said anything of the kind and I
suspect you would never give it a thought.

TOM: Don't be so suspicious of me.

AMANDA: At least I hope he's the type that's up and coming.

TOM: I think he really goes in for self-improvement.

AMANDA: What reason have you to think so?

TOM: He goes to night school.

AMANDA [*beaming*]: Splendid! What does he do, I mean
study?

TOM: Radio engineering and public speaking!

AMANDA: Then he has visions of being advanced in the
world! Any young man who studies public speaking is
aiming to have an executive job some day!

And radio engineering? A thing for the future!
Both of these facts are very illuminating. Those are the
sort of things that a mother should know concerning any
young man who comes to call on her daughter. Seriously
or – not.

TOM: One little warning. He doesn't know about Laura. I
didn't let on that we had dark ulterior motives. I just said,
why don't you come and have dinner with us? He said
okay and that was the whole conversation.

AMANDA: I bet it was! You're eloquent as an oyster.
However, he'll know about Laura when he gets here.
When he sees how lovely and sweet and pretty she is, he'll
thank his lucky stars he was asked to dinner.

TOM: Mother, you mustn't expect too much of Laura.

AMANDA: What do you mean?

TOM: Laura seems all those things to you and me because
she's ours and we love her. We don't even notice she's
crippled any more. — *Suggests Laura is diff to other girl*

AMANDA: Don't say crippled! You know that I never
allow that word to be used! *She shy*

TOM: But face facts, Mother. She is and – that's not all – *Sta alo*

AMANDA: What do you mean 'not all'?

TOM: Laura is very different from other girls.

AMANDA: I think the difference is all to her advantage.

TOM: Not quite all – in the eyes of others – strangers – she's
terribly shy and lives in a world of her own and those
things make her seem a little peculiar to people outside
the house. *strange*

AMANDA: Don't say peculiar.

TOM: Face the facts. She is.

[THE DANCE-HALL MUSIC CHANGES TO A TANGO
THAT HAS A MINOR AND SOMEWHAT OMINOUS
TONE.]

AMANDA: In what way is she peculiar – may I ask?

TOM [*gently*]: She lives in a world of her own – a world of –

little glass ornaments, Mother. ... [*Gets up.* AMANDA *remains holding brush, looking at him, troubled.*] She plays old phonograph records and – that's about all – [*He glances at himself in the mirror and crosses to door.*]

AMANDA [*sharply*]: Where are you going?

TOM: I'm going to the movies. [*Out screen door.*]

AMANDA: Not to the movies, every night to the movies! [*Follows quickly to screen door.*] I don't believe you always go to the movies! [*He is gone.* AMANDA *looks worriedly after him for a moment. Then vitality and optimism return and she turns from the door. Crossing to portières.*] Laura! Laura! [LAURA *answers from kitchenette.*]

LAURA: Yes, Mother.

AMANDA: Let those dishes go and come in front! [LAURA *appears with dish towel. Gaily.*] Laura, come here and make a wish on the moon!

    [SCREEN IMAGE: MOON.]

LAURA [*entering*]: Moon – moon?

AMANDA: A little silver slipper of a moon.

Look over your left shoulder, Laura, and make a wish!

    [LAURA *looks faintly puzzled as if called out of sleep.* AMANDA *seizes her shoulders and turns her at an angle by the door.*]

Now!

Now, darling, *wish*!

LAURA: What shall I wish for, Mother?

AMANDA [*her voice trembling and her eyes suddenly filling with tears*]: Happiness! Good fortune!

    [*The violin rises and the stage dims out.*]

CURTAIN

SCENE SIX

[IMAGE: HIGH SCHOOL HERO.]

TOM: And so the following evening I brought Jim home to dinner. I had known Jim slightly in high school. In high school Jim was a hero. He had tremendous Irish good nature and vitality with the scrubbed and polished look of white chinaware. He seemed to move in a continual spotlight. He was a star in basket-ball, captain of the debating club, president of the senior class and the glee club and he sang the male lead in the annual light operas. He was always running or bounding, never just walking. He seemed always at the point of defeating the law of gravity. He was shooting with such velocity through his adolescence that you would logically expect him to arrive at nothing short of the White House by the time he was thirty. But Jim apparently ran into more interference after his graduation from Soldan. His speed had definitely slowed. Six years after he left high school he was holding a job that wasn't much better than mine.

[IMAGE: CLERK.]

He was the only one at the warehouse with whom I was on friendly terms. I was valuable to him as someone who could remember his former glory, who had seen him win basketball games and the silver cup in debating. He knew of my secret practice of retiring to a cabinet of the washroom to work on poems when business was slack in the warehouse. He called me Shakespeare. And while the other boys in the warehouse regarded me with suspicious hostility, Jim took a humorous attitude toward me. Gradually his attitude affected the others, their hostility wore off and they also began to smile at me as people smile at an oddly fashioned dog who trots across their path at some distance.

I knew that Jim and Laura had known each other at Soldan, and I had heard Laura speak admiringly of his voice. I didn't know if Jim remembered her or not. In high school Laura had been as unobtrusive as Jim had been astonishing. If he did remember Laura, it was not as my sister, for when I asked him to dinner, he grinned and said, 'You know, Shakespeare, I never thought of you as having folks !'

He was about to discover that I did. . . .

[LIGHT UPSTAGE.

   LEGEND ON SCREEN: 'THE ACCENT OF A COMING FOOT'.

Friday evening. It is about five o'clock of a late spring evening which comes 'scattering poems in the sky'.

A delicate lemony light is in the Wingfield apartment.

AMANDA *has worked like a Turk in preparation for the gentleman caller. The results are astonishing. The new floor lamp with its rose-silk shade is in place, a coloured paper lantern conceals the broken light fixture in the ceiling, new billowing white curtains are at the windows, chintz covers are on chairs and sofa, a pair of new sofa pillows make their initial appearance.*

Open boxes and tissue paper are scattered on the floor.

LAURA *stands in the middle with lifted arms while* AMANDA *crouches before her, adjusting the hem of the new dress, devout and ritualistic. The dress is coloured and designed by memory. The arrangement of* LAURA'S *hair is changed; it is softer and more becoming. A fragile, unearthly prettiness has come out in* LAURA: *she is like a piece of translucent glass touched by light, given a momentary radiance, not actual, not lasting.*]

AMANDA [*impatiently*]: Why are you trembling?

LAURA: Mother, you've made me so nervous!

AMANDA: How have I made you nervous?

LAURA: By all this fuss! You make it seem so important!

AMANDA: I don't understand you, Laura. You couldn't be satisfied with just sitting home, and yet whenever I try to arrange something for you, you seem to resist it. [*She gets up.*]
Now take a look at yourself.
No, wait! Wait just a moment – I have an idea!

LAURA: What is it now?

[AMANDA *produces two powder puffs which she wraps in handkerchiefs and stuffs in* LAURA'S *bosom.*]

LAURA: Mother, what are you doing?

AMANDA: They call them 'Gay Deceivers'!

LAURA: I won't wear them!

AMANDA: You will!

LAURA: Why should I?

AMANDA: Because, to be painfully honest, your chest is flat.

LAURA: You make it seem like we were setting a trap.

AMANDA: All pretty girls are a trap, a pretty trap, and men expect them to be!

[LEGEND: 'A PRETTY TRAP'.]

Now look at yourself, young lady. This is the prettiest you will ever be!
I've got to fix myself now! You're going to be surprised by your mother's appearance! [*She crosses through portières, humming gaily.*]

[LAURA *moves slowly to the long mirror and stares solemnly at herself. A wind blows the white curtains inward in a slow, graceful motion and with a faint, sorrowful sighing.*]

AMANDA [*off stage*]: It isn't dark enough yet. [LAURA *turns slowly before the mirror with a troubled look.*]

[LEGEND ON SCREEN: 'THIS IS MY SISTER: CELE-
BRATE HER WITH STRINGS!' MUSIC.]

AMANDA [*laughing, off*]: I'm going to show you something.
I'm going to make a spectacular appearance!
LAURA: What is it, Mother?
AMANDA: Possess your soul in patience – you will see!
Something I've resurrected from that old trunk! Styles
haven't changed so terribly much after all. . . .

[*She parts the portières.*]

Now just look at your mother!

[*She wears a girlish frock of yellowed voile with a blue silk
sash. She carries a bunch of jonquils – the legend of her youth
is nearly revived.*]

[*Feverishly*]: This is the dress in which I led the cotillion,
won the cakewalk twice at Sunset Hill, wore one spring
to the Governor's ball in Jackson!
See how I sashayed around the ballroom, Laura?

[*She raises her skirt and does a mincing step around the room.*]

I wore it on Sundays for my gentlemen callers! I had it on
the day I met your father –
I had malaria fever all that spring. The change of climate
from East Tennessee to the Delta – weakened resistance –
I had a little temperature all the time – not enough to be
serious – just enough to make me restless and giddy! –
Invitations poured in – parties all over the Delta! – 'Stay
in bed,' said mother, 'you have fever!' – but I just
wouldn't. – I took quinine but kept on going, going! –
Evenings, dances! – Afternoons, long, long rides! Picnics
– lovely! – So lovely, that country in May. – All lacy with
dogwood, literally flooded with jonquils! – That was the
spring I had the craze for jonquils. Jonquils became an
absolute obsession. Mother said, 'Honey, there's no more
room for jonquils.' And still I kept on bringing in more

jonquils. Whenever, wherever I saw them, I'd say, 'Stop! Stop! I see jonquils!' I made the young men help me gather the jonquils! It was a joke, Amanda and her jonquils! Finally there were no more vases to hold them, every available space was filled with jonquils. No vases to hold them? All right, I'll hold them myself! And then I – [*She stops in front of the picture.* MUSIC.] met your father! Malaria fever and jonquils and then – this – boy. . . .

[*She switches on the rose-coloured lamp.*]

I hope they get here before it starts to rain.

[*She crosses upstage and places the jonquils in bowl on table.*]

I gave your brother a little extra change so he and Mr O'Connor could take the service car home.

LAURA [*with altered look*]: What did you say his name was?

AMANDA: O'Connor.

LAURA: What is his first name?

AMANDA: I don't remember. Oh, yes, I do. It was – Jim!

[LAURA *sways slightly and catches hold of a chair.*
    LEGEND ON SCREEN: 'NOT JIM!']

LAURA [*faintly*]: Not – Jim!

AMANDA: Yes, that was it, it was Jim! I've never known a Jim that wasn't nice!

[MUSIC OMINOUS.]

LAURA: Are you sure his name is Jim O'Connor?

AMANDA: Yes. Why?

LAURA: Is he the one that Tom used to know in high school?

AMANDA: He didn't say so. I think he just got to know him at the warehouse.

LAURA: There was a Jim O'Connor we both knew in high school – [*Then, with effort.*] If that is the one that Tom is bringing to dinner – you'll have to excuse me, I won't come to the table.

AMANDA: What sort of nonsense is this?

LAURA: You asked me once if I'd ever liked a boy. Don't you remember I showed you this boy's picture?

AMANDA: You mean the boy you showed me in the year book?

LAURA: Yes, that boy.

AMANDA: Laura, Laura, were you in love with that boy?

LAURA: I don't know, Mother. All I know is I couldn't sit at the table if it was him!

AMANDA: It won't be him! It isn't the least bit likely. But whether it is or not, you will come to the table. You will not be excused.

LAURA: I'll have to be, Mother.

AMANDA: I don't intend to humour your silliness, Laura. I've had too much from you and your brother, both!
So just sit down and compose yourself till they come. Tom has forgotten his key so you'll have to let them in, when they arrive.

LAURA [*panicky*]: Oh, Mother – *you* answer the door!

AMANDA [*lightly*]: I'll be in the kitchen – busy!

LAURA: Oh, Mother, please answer the door, don't make me do it!

AMANDA [*crossing into kitchenette*]: I've got to fix the dressing for the salmon. Fuss, fuss – silliness! over a gentleman caller!

[*Door swings shut.* LAURA *is left alone.*

LEGEND: 'TERROR!'

She utters a low moan and turns off the lamp – sits stiffly on the edge of the sofa, knotting her fingers together.

LEGEND ON SCREEN: 'THE OPENING OF A DOOR!'

TOM *and* JIM *appear on the fire-escape steps and climb to landing. Hearing their approach,* LAURA *rises with a panicky gesture. She retreats to the portières.*

The doorbell. LAURA *catches her breath and touches her throat. Low drums.*]

AMANDA [*calling*]: Laura, sweetheart! The door!

[LAURA *stares at it without moving.*]

JIM: I think we just beat the rain.

TOM: Uh-huh. [*He rings again, nervously.* JIM· *whistles and fishes for a cigarette.*]

AMANDA [*very, very gaily*]: Laura, that is your brother and Mr O'Connor! Will you let them in, darling?

[LAURA *crosses toward kitchenette door.*]

LAURA [*breathlessly*]: Mother – you go to the door!

[AMANDA *steps out of kitchenette and stares furiously at* LAURA. *She points imperiously at the door.*]

LAURA: Please, please!

AMANDA [*in a fierce whisper*]: What is the matter with you, you silly thing?

LAURA [*desperately*]: Please, you answer it, *please*!

AMANDA: I told you I wasn't going to humour you, Laura. Why have you chosen this moment to lose your mind?

LAURA: Please, please, please, you go!

AMANDA: You'll have to go to the door because I can't!

LAURA [*despairingly*]: I can't either!

AMANDA: *Why?*

LAURA: I'm *sick*!

AMANDA: I'm sick, too – of your nonsense! Why can't you and your brother be normal people? Fantastic whims and behaviour!

[TOM *gives a long ring.*]

Preposterous goings on! Can you give me one reason – [*Calls out lyrically.*] COMING! JUST ONE SECOND! – why you should be afraid to open a door? Now you answer it, Laura!

LAURA: Oh, oh, oh . . . [*She returns through the portières. Darts to the victrola and winds it frantically and turns it on.*]

AMANDA: Laura Wingfield, you march right to that door!

LAURA: Yes – yes, Mother!

[*A faraway, scratchy rendition of 'Dardanella' softens the air and gives her strength to move through it. She slips to the door and draws it cautiously open.*

TOM *enters with the caller,* JIM O'CONNOR.]

TOM: Laura, this is Jim. Jim, this is my sister, Laura.

JIM [*stepping inside*]: I didn't know that Shakespeare had a sister!

LAURA [*retreating stiff and trembling from the door*]: How – how do you do?

JIM [*heartily extending his hand*]: Okay!

[LAURA *touches it hesitantly with hers.*]

JIM: Your hand's *cold*, Laura!

LAURA: Yes, well – I've been playing the victrola. . . .

JIM: Must have been playing classical music on it! You ought to play a little hot swing music to warm you up!

LAURA: Excuse me – I haven't finished playing the victrola. . . . [*She turns awkwardly and hurries into the front room. She pauses a second by the victrola. Then catches her breath and darts through the portières like a frightened deer.*]

JIM [*grinning*]: What was the matter?

TOM: Oh – with Laura? Laura is – terribly shy.

JIM: Shy, huh? It's unusual to meet a shy girl nowadays. I don't believe you ever mentioned you had a sister.

TOM: Well, now you know. I have one. Here is the *Post Dispatch*. You want a piece of it?

JIM: Uh-huh.

TOM: What piece? The comics?

JIM: Sports! [*Glances at it.*] Ole Dizzy Dean is on his bad behaviour.

TOM [*disinterested*]: Yeah? [*Lights cigarette and crosses back to fire-escape door.*]

JIM: Where are *you* going?

TOM: I'm going out on the terrace.

JIM [*goes after him*]: You know, Shakespeare – I'm going to sell you a bill of goods!

TOM: What goods?

JIM: A course I'm taking.

TOM: Huh?

JIM: In public speaking! You and me, we're not the warehouse type.

TOM: Thanks – that's good news.
But what has public speaking got to do with it?

JIM: It fits you for – executive positions!

TOM: Awww.

JIM: I tell you it's done a helluva lot for me.

[IMAGE: EXECUTIVE AT DESK.]

TOM: In what respect?

JIM: In every! Ask yourself what is the difference between you an' me and men in the office down front? Brains? – No! – Ability? – No! Then what? Just one little thing –

TOM: What is that one little thing?

JIM: Primarily it amounts to – social poise! Being able to square up to people and hold your own on any social level!

AMANDA [*off stage*]: Tom?

TOM: Yes, Mother?

AMANDA: Is that you and Mr O'Connor?

TOM: Yes, Mother.

AMANDA: Well, you just make yourselves comfortable in there.

TOM: Yes, Mother.

AMANDA: Ask Mr O'Connor if he would like to wash his hands.

JIM: Aw, no – no – thank you – I took care of that at the warehouse. Tom –

TOM: Yes?

JIM: Mr Mendoza was speaking to me about you.

TOM: Favourably?

JIM: What do you think?

TOM: Well –

JIM: You're going to be out of a job if you don't wake up.

TOM: I am waking up –

JIM: You show no signs.

TOM: The signs are interior.

[IMAGE ON SCREEN: THE SAILING VESSEL WITH JOLLY ROGER AGAIN.]

TOM: I'm planning to change. [*He leans over the rail speaking with quiet exhilaration. The incandescent marquees and signs of the first-run movie houses light his face from across the alley. He looks like a voyager.*] I'm right at the point of committing myself to a future that doesn't include the warehouse and Mr Mendoza or even a night-school course in public speaking.

JIM: What are you gassing about?

TOM: I'm tired of the movies.

JIM: Movies!

TOM: Yes, movies! Look at them – [*A wave toward the marvels of Grand Avenue.*] All of those glamorous people – having adventures – hogging it all, gobbling the whole thing up! You know what happens? People go to the *movies* instead of *moving*! Hollywood characters are supposed to have all the adventures for everybody in America, while everybody in America sits in a dark room and watches them have them! Yes, until there's a war. That's when adventure becomes available to the masses! *Everyone's* dish, not only Gable's! Then the people in the dark room come out of the dark room to have some adventure themselves – Goody, goody! – It's our turn now, to go to the South Sea

people go to movies to see adventure-
they do not a lot of adventure in
America

Islands – to make a safari – to be exotic, far-off! – But I'm not patient. I don't want to wait till then. I'm tired of the *movies* and I am *about to move*!

JIM [*incredulously*]: Move?

TOM: Yes.

JIM: When?

TOM: Soon!

JIM: Where? Where?

> [THEME THREE MUSIC SEEMS TO ANSWER THE QUESTION, WHILE TOM THINKS IT OVER. HE SEARCHES AMONG HIS POCKETS.]

TOM: I'm starting to boil inside. I know I seem dreamy, but inside – well, I'm boiling! – Whenever I pick up a shoe, I shudder a little thinking how short life is and what I am doing! – Whatever that means, I know it doesn't mean shoes – except as something to wear on a traveller's feet! [*Finds paper.*] Look –

JIM: What?

TOM: I'm a member.

JIM [*reading*]: The Union of Merchant Seamen.

TOM: I paid my dues this month, instead of the light bill.

JIM: You will regret it when they turn the lights off.

TOM: I won't be here.

JIM: How about your mother?

TOM: I'm like my father. The bastard son of a bastard! See how he grins? And he's been absent going on sixteen years!

JIM: You're just talking, you drip. How does your mother feel about it?

TOM: Shhh! – Here comes mother! Mother is not acquainted with my plans!

AMANDA [*enters portières*]: Where are you all?

TOM: On the terrace, Mother.

> [*They start inside. She advances to them.* TOM *is distinctly*

shocked at her appearance. Even JIM *blinks a little. He is making his first contact with girlish Southern vivacity and in spite of the night-school course in public speaking is somewhat thrown off the beam by the unexpected outlay of social charm.*

Certain responses are attempted by JIM *but are swept aside by* AMANDA'S *gay laughter and chatter.* TOM *is embarrassed but after the first shock* JIM *reacts very warmly. Grins and chuckles, is altogether won over.*

[IMAGE: AMANDA AS A GIRL.]

AMANDA [*coyly smiling, shaking her girlish ringlets*]: Well, well, well, so this is Mr O'Connor. Introductions entirely unnecessary. I've heard so much about you from my boy. I finally said to him, Tom – good gracious! – why don't you bring this paragon to supper? I'd like to meet this nice young man at the warehouse! – Instead of just hearing you sing his praises so much!

I don't know why my son is so stand-offish – that's not Southern behaviour!

Let's sit down and – I think we could stand a little more air in here! Tom, leave the door open. I felt a nice fresh breeze a moment ago. Where has it gone to?

Mmm, so warm already! And not quite summer, even. We're going to burn up when summer really gets started. However, we're having – we're having a very light supper. I think light things are better fo' this time of year. The same as light clothes are. Light clothes an' light food are what warm weather calls fo'. You know our blood gets so thick during th' winter – it takes a while fo' us to *adjust* ou'selves! – when the season changes ...

It's come so quick this year. I wasn't prepared. All of a sudden – heavens! Already summer! – I ran to the trunk an' pulled out this light dress – Terribly old! Historical almost! But feels so good – so good an' co-ol, y' know. ....

TOM: Mother –

AMANDA: Yes, honey?

TOM: How about – supper?

AMANDA: Honey, you go ask Sister if supper is ready! You know that Sister is in full charge of supper! Tell her you hungry boys are waiting for it.

[*To* JIM.]

Have you met Laura?

JIM: She –

AMANDA: Let you in? Oh, good, you've met already! It's rare for a girl as sweet an' pretty as Laura to be domestic! But Laura is, thank heavens, not only pretty but also very domestic. I'm not at all. I never was a bit. I never could make a thing but angel-food cake. Well, in the South we had so many servants. Gone, gone, gone. All vestige of gracious living! Gone completely! I wasn't prepared for what the future brought me. All of my gentlemen callers were sons of planters and so of course I assumed that I would be married to one and raise my family on a large piece of land with plenty of servants. But man proposes – and woman accepts the proposal! – To vary that old, old saying a little bit – I married no planter! I married a man who worked for the telephone company! – That gallantly smiling gentleman over there! [*Points to the picture.*] A telephone man who – fell in love with long distance! – Now he travels and I don't even know where! – But what am I going on for about my – tribulations? Tell me yours – I hope you don't have any! Tom?

TOM [*returning*]: Yes, Mother?

AMANDA: Is supper nearly ready?

TOM: It looks to me like supper is on the table.

AMANDA: Let me look – [*She rises prettily and looks through portières.*] Oh, lovely! – But where is Sister?

TOM: Laura is not feeling well and she says that she thinks she'd better not come to the table.

AMANDA: What? – Nonsense! – Laura? Oh, Laura!

LAURA [*off stage, faintly*]: Yes, Mother.

AMANDA: You really must come to the table. We won't be seated until you come to the table!

Come in, Mr O'Connor. You sit over there, and I'll –
Laura? Laura Wingfield!

You're keeping us waiting, honey! We can't say grace until you come to the table!

> [*The back door is pushed weakly open and* LAURA *comes in. She is obviously quite faint, her lips trembling, her eyes wide and staring. She moves unsteadily toward the table.*
>
> LEGEND: 'TERROR!'
>
> *Outside a summer storm is coming abruptly. The white curtains billow inward at the windows and there is a sorrowful murmur and deep blue dusk.*
>
> LAURA *suddenly stumbles – she catches at a chair with a faint moan.*]

TOM: Laura!

AMANDA: Laura!

> [*There is a clap of thunder.*
>
> LEGEND: 'AH!']

[*Despairingly*] Why, Laura, you *are* sick, darling! Tom, help your sister into the living-room, dear!

Sit in the living-room, Laura – rest on the sofa.

Well!

> [*To the gentleman caller.*]

Standing over the hot stove made her ill! – I told her that was just too warm this evening, but –

> [TOM *comes back in.* LAURA *is on the sofa.*]

Is Laura all right now?

TOM: Yes.

AMANDA: What *is* that? Rain? A nice cool rain has come up!

[*She gives the gentleman caller a frightened look.*]

I think we may – have grace – now ...

[TOM *looks at her steadily.*]

Tom, honey – you say grace!
TOM: Oh ...
'For these and all thy mercies –'

[*They bow their heads,* AMANDA *stealing a nervous glance at* JIM. *In the living-room* LAURA, *stretched on the sofa, clenches her hand to her lips, to hold back a shuddering sob.*]

God's Holy Name be praised –
THE SCENE DIMS OUT

SCENE SEVEN

A SOUVENIR

Half an hour later. Dinner is just being finished in the upstage area which is concealed by the drawn portières.

[*As the curtain rises* LAURA *is still huddled upon the sofa, her feet drawn under her, her head resting on a pale blue pillow, her eyes wide and mysteriously watchful. The new floor lamp with its shade of rose-coloured silk gives a soft, becoming light to her face, bringing out the fragile, unearthly prettiness which usually escapes attention. There is a steady murmur of rain, but it is slackening and stops soon after the scene begins; the air outside becomes pale and luminous as the moon breaks out. A moment after the curtain rises, the lights in both rooms flicker and go out.*]

JIM: Hey, there, Mr Light Bulb!

[AMANDA *laughs nervously.*

LEGEND: 'SUSPENSION OF A PUBLIC SERVICE'.]

AMANDA: Where was Moses when the lights went out? Ha-ha. Do you know the answer to that one, Mr O'Connor?

JIM: No, Ma'am, what's the answer?

AMANDA: In the dark!

[JIM *laughs appreciatively.*]

Everybody sit still. I'll light the candles. Isn't it lucky we have them on the table? Where's a match? Which of you gentlemen can provide a match?

JIM: Here.

AMANDA: Thank you, sir.

JIM: Not at all, Ma'am!

AMANDA: I guess the fuse has burnt out. Mr O'Connor,

can you tell a burnt-out fuse? I know I can't and Tom is a
total loss when it comes to mechanics.

[SOUND: GETTING UP: VOICES RECEDE A LITTLE
TO KITCHENETTE.]

Oh, be careful you don't bump into something. We don't
want our gentleman caller to break his neck. Now
wouldn't that be a fine howdy-do?

JIM: Ha-ha!

Where is the fuse-box?

AMANDA: Right here next to the stove. Can you see anything?

JIM: Just a minute.

AMANDA: Isn't electricity a mysterious thing?
Wasn't it Benjamin Franklin who tied a key to a kite?
We live in such a mysterious universe, don't we? Some
people say that science clears up all the mysteries for us.
In my opinion it only creates more!
Have you found it yet?

JIM: No, Ma'am. All these fuses look okay to me.

AMANDA: Tom!

TOM: Yes, Mother?

AMANDA: That light bill I gave you several days ago. The
one I told you we got the notices about?

[LEGEND: 'HA!']

TOM: Oh. – Yeah.

AMANDA: You didn't neglect to pay it by any chance?

TOM: Why, I –

AMANDA: Didn't! I might have known it!

JIM: Shakespeare probably wrote a poem on that light bill,
Mrs Wingfield.

AMANDA: I might have known better than to trust him
with it! There's such a high price for negligence in this
world!

JIM: Maybe the poem will win a ten-dollar prize.

AMANDA: We'll just have to spend the remainder of the evening in the nineteenth century, before Mr Edison made the Mazda lamp!

JIM: Candlelight is my favourite kind of light.

AMANDA: That shows you're romantic! But that's no excuse for Tom.

Well, we got through dinner. Very considerate of them to let us get through dinner before they plunged us into ever-lasting darkness, wasn't it, Mr O'Connor?

JIM: Ha-ha!

AMANDA: Tom, as a penalty for your carelessness you can help me with the dishes.

JIM: Let me give you a hand.

AMANDA: Indeed you will not!

JIM: I ought to be good for something.

AMANDA: Good for something? [*Her tone is rhapsodic.*] *You?* Why, Mr O'Connor, nobody, *nobody*'s given me this much entertainment in years – as you have!

JIM: Aw, now, Mrs Wingfield!

AMANDA: I'm not exaggerating, not one bit! But Sister is all by her lonesome. You go keep her company in the parlour! I'll give you this lovely old candelabrum that used to be on the altar at the church of the Heavenly Rest. It was melted a little out of shape when the church burnt down. Lightning struck it one spring.

Gypsy Jones was holding a revival at the time and he intimated that the church was destroyed because the Episcopalians gave card parties.

JIM: Ha-ha.

AMANDA: And how about you coaxing Sister to drink a little wine? I think it would be good for her! Can you carry both at once?

JIM: Sure. I'm Superman!

AMANDA: Now, Thomas, get into this apron!

[*The door of kitchenette swings closed on* AMANDA'S *gay*

laughter; the flickering light approaches the portières.

LAURA sits up nervously as he enters. Her speech at first is low and breathless from the almost intolerable strain of being alone with a stranger.

THE LEGEND: 'I DON'T SUPPOSE YOU REMEMBER ME AT ALL!'

In her first speeches in this scene, before JIM's warmth overcomes her paralysing shyness, LAURA's voice is thin and breathless as though she has just run up a steep flight of stairs.

JIM's attitude is gently humorous. In playing this scene it should be stressed that while the incident is apparently unimportant, it is to LAURA the climax of her secret life.]

JIM: Hello, there, Laura.

LAURA [*faintly*]: Hello. [*She clears her throat.*]

JIM: How are you feeling now? Better?

LAURA: Yes. Yes, thank you.

JIM: This is for you. A little dandelion wine. [*He extends it toward her with extravagant gallantry.*]

LAURA: Thank you.

JIM: Drink it – but don't get drunk!

[*He laughs heartily.* LAURA *takes the glass uncertainly; laughs shyly.*]

Where shall I set the candles?

LAURA: Oh – oh, anywhere. . . .

JIM: How about here on the floor? Any objections?

LAURA: No.

JIM: I'll spread a newspaper under to catch the drippings. I like to sit on the floor. Mind if I do?

LAURA: Oh, no.

JIM: Give me a pillow?

LAURA: What?

JIM: A pillow!

LAURA: Oh . . . [*Hands him one quickly.*]

JIM: How about you? Don't you like to sit on the floor?

LAURA: Oh – yes.

JIM: Why don't you, then?

LAURA: I – will.

JIM: Take a pillow! [LAURA *does. Sits on the other side of the candelabrum.* JIM *crosses his legs and smiles engagingly at her.*] I can't hardly see you sitting way over there.

LAURA: I can – see you.

JIM: I know, but that's not fair, I'm in the limelight. [LAURA *moves her pillow closer.*] Good! Now I can see you! Comfortable?

LAURA: Yes.

JIM: So am I. Comfortable as a cow! Will you have some gum?

LAURA: No, thank you.

JIM: I think that I will indulge, with your permission. [*Musingly unwraps it and holds it up.*] Think of the fortune made by the guy that invented the first piece of chewing gum. Amazing, huh? The Wrigley Building is one of the sights of Chicago. – I saw it summer before last when I went up to the Century of Progress. Did you take in the Century of Progress?

LAURA: No, I didn't.

JIM: Well, it was quite a wonderful exposition. What impressed me most was the Hall of Science. Gives you an idea of what the future will be in America, even more wonderful than the present time is! [*Pause. Smiling at her.*] Your brother tells me you're shy. Is that right, Laura?

LAURA: I – don't know.

JIM: I judge you to be an old-fashioned type of girl. Well, I think that's a pretty good type to be. Hope you don't think I'm being too personal – do you?

LAURA [*hastily, out of embarrassment*]: I believe I will take a piece of gum, if you – don't mind. [*Clearing her throat.*] Mr O'Connor, have you – kept up with your singing?

JIM: Singing? Me?

LAURA: Yes. I remember what a beautiful voice you had.

JIM: When did you hear me sing?

[VOICE OFF STAGE IN THE PAUSE]

VOICE [*off stage*]:

> O blow, ye winds, heigh-ho,
> A-roving I will go!
> I'm off to my love
> With a boxing glove –
> Ten thousand miles away!

JIM: You say you've heard me sing?

LAURA: Oh, yes! Yes, very often ... I don't suppose – you remember me – at all?

JIM [*smiling doubtfully*]: You know I have an idea I've seen you before. I had that idea soon as you opened the door. It seemed almost like I was about to remember your name. But the name that I started to call you – wasn't a name! And so I stopped myself before I said it.

LAURA: Wasn't it – Blue Roses?

JIM [*springs up. Grinning*]: Blue Roses! – My gosh, yes – Blue Roses! That's what I had on my tongue when you opened the door!

Isn't it funny what tricks your memory plays? I didn't connect you with high school somehow or other.

But that's where it was; it was high school. I didn't even know you were Shakespeare's sister!

Gosh, I'm sorry.

LAURA: I didn't expect you to. You – barely knew me!

JIM: But we did have a speaking acquaintance, huh?

LAURA: Yes, we – spoke to each other.

JIM: When did you recognize me?

LAURA: Oh, right away!

JIM: Soon as I came in the door?

LAURA: When I heard your name I thought it was probably you. I knew that Tom used to know you a little in high school. So when you came in the door –

Well, then I was – sure.

JIM: Why didn't you *say* something, then?

LAURA [*breathlessly*]: I didn't know what to say, I was – too surprised!

JIM: For goodness' sakes! You know, this sure is funny!

LAURA: Yes! Yes, isn't it, though ...

JIM: Didn't we have a class in something together?

LAURA: Yes, we did.

JIM: What class was that?

LAURA: It was – singing – Chorus!

JIM: Aw!

LAURA: I sat across the aisle from you in the Aud.

JIM: Aw.

LAURA: Mondays, Wednesday, and Fridays.

JIM: Now I remember – you always came in late.

LAURA: Yes, it was so hard for me, getting upstairs. I had that brace on my leg – it clumped so loud!

JIM: I never heard any clumping.

LAURA [*wincing at the recollection*]: To me it sounded like – thunder!

JIM: Well, well, well, I never even noticed.

LAURA: And everybody was seated before I came in. I had to walk in front of all those people. My seat was in the back row. I had to go clumping all the way up the aisle with everyone watching!

JIM: You shouldn't have been self-conscious.

LAURA: I know, but I was. It was always such a relief when the singing started.

JIM: Aw, yes, I've placed you now! I used to call you Blue Roses. How was it that I got started calling you that?

LAURA: I was out of school a little while with pleurosis. When I came back you asked me what was the matter. I said I had pleurosis – you thought I said Blue Roses. That's what you always called me after that!

JIM: I hope you didn't mind.

LAURA: Oh, no – I liked it. You see, I wasn't acquainted with many – people. ...

JIM: As I remember you sort of stuck by yourself.

LAURA: I – I – never have had much luck at – making friends.

JIM: I don't see why you wouldn't.

LAURA: Well, I – started out badly.

JIM: You mean being –

LAURA: Yes, it sort of – stood between me –

JIM: You shouldn't have let it!

LAURA: I know, but it did, and –

JIM: You were shy with people!

LAURA: I tried not to be but never could –

JIM: Overcome it?

LAURA: No, I – I never could!

JIM: I guess being shy is something you have to work out of kind of gradually.

LAURA [*sorrowfully*]: Yes – I guess it –

JIM: Takes time!

LAURA: Yes –

JIM: People are not so dreadful when you know them. That's what you have to remember! And everybody has problems, not just you, but practically everybody has got some problems.

You think of yourself as having the only problems, as being the only one who is disappointed. But just look around you and you will see lots of people as disappointed as you are. For instance, I hoped when I was going to high school that I would be further along at this time, six years later, than I am now – You remember that wonderful write-up I had in *The Torch*?

LAURA: Yes! [*She rises and crosses to table.*]

JIM: It said I was bound to succeed in anything I went into! [LAURA *returns with the annual.*] Holy Jeez! *The Torch!* [*He accepts it reverently. They smile across it with mutual wonder.* LAURA *crouches beside him and they begin to turn through it.* LAURA'S *shyness is dissolving in his warmth.*]

LAURA: Here you are in *The Pirates of Penzance!*

JIM: [*wistfully*]: I sang the baritone lead in that operetta.

LAURA [*raptly*]: So – beautifully !

JIM [*protesting*]: Aw –

LAURA: Yes, yes – beautifully – beautifully !

JIM: You heard me?

LAURA: All three times !

JIM: No !

LAURA: Yes !

JIM: All three performances?

LAURA [*looking down*]: Yes.

JIM: Why?

LAURA: I – wanted to ask you to – autograph my programme.

JIM: Why didn't you ask me to?

LAURA: You were always surrounded by your own friends so much that I never had a chance to.

JIM: You should have just –

LAURA: Well, I – thought you might think I was –

JIM: Thought I might think you was – what?

LAURA: Oh –

JIM [*with reflective relish*]: I was beleaguered by females in those days.

LAURA: You were terribly popular !

JIM: Yeah –

LAURA: You had such a – friendly way –

JIM: I was spoiled in high school.

LAURA: Everybody – liked you !

JIM: Including you?

LAURA: I – yes, I – I did, too – [*She gently closes the book in her lap.*]

JIM: Well, well, well ! – Give me that programme, Laura. [*She hands it to him. He signs it with a flourish.*] There you are – better late than never !

LAURA: Oh, I – what a – surprise !

JIM: My signature isn't worth very much right now. But some day – maybe – it will increase in value !

Being disappointed is one thing and being discouraged is
something else. I am disappointed but I am not discouraged. I'm twenty-three years old.

How old are you?

LAURA: I'll be twenty-four in June.

JIM: That's not old age!

LAURA: No, but –

JIM: You finished high school?

LAURA [with difficulty]: I didn't go back.

JIM: You mean you dropped out?

LAURA: I made bad grades in my final examinations. [She
rises and replaces the book and the programme. Her voice
strained.] How is – Emily Meisenbach getting along?

JIM: Oh, that kraut-head!

LAURA: Why do you call her that?

JIM: That's what she was.

LAURA: You're not still – going with her?

JIM: I never see her.

LAURA: It said in the Personal Section that you were –
engaged!

JIM: I know, but I wasn't impressed by that – propaganda!

LAURA: It wasn't – the truth?

JIM: Only in Emily's optimistic opinion!

LAURA: Oh –

[LEGEND: 'WHAT HAVE YOU DONE SINCE HIGH
SCHOOL?'
    JIM lights a cigarette and leans indolently back on his elbows
smiling at LAURA with a warmth and charm which lights her
inwardly with altar candles. She remains by the table and turns
in her hands a piece of glass to cover her tumult.]

JIM [after several reflective puffs on a cigarette]: What have you
done since high school? [She seems not to hear him.] Huh?
[LAURA looks up.] I said what have you done since high
school, Laura?

LAURA: Nothing much.

JIM: You must have been doing something these six long years.

LAURA: Yes.

JIM: Well, then, such as what?

LAURA: I took a business course at business college –

JIM: How did that work out?

LAURA: Well, not very – well – I had to drop out, it gave me – indigestion –

[JIM *laughs gently*.]

JIM: What are you doing now?

LAURA: I don't do anything – much. Oh, please don't think I sit around doing nothing! My glass collection takes up a good deal of time. Glass is something you have to take good care of.

JIM: What did you say – about glass?

LAURA: Collection I said – I have one – [*She clears her throat and turns away, acutely shy.*]

JIM [*abruptly*]: You know what I judge to be the trouble with you?

Inferiority complex! Know what that is? That's what they call it when someone low-rates himself!

I understand it because I had it, too. Although my case was not so aggravated as yours seems to be. I had it until I took up public speaking, developed my voice, and learned that I had an aptitude for science. Before that time I never thought of myself as being outstanding in any way whatsoever!

Now I've never made a regular study of it, but I have a friend who says I can analyse people better than doctors that make a profession of it. I don't claim that to be necessarily true, but I can sure guess a person's psychology, Laura! [*Takes out his gum.*] Excuse me, Laura. I always take it out when the flavour is gone. I'll use this scrap of paper to wrap it in. I know how it is to get it stuck on a shoe.

Yep – that's what I judge to be your principal trouble. A lack of amount of faith in yourself as a person. You don't have the proper amount of faith in yourself. I'm basing that fact on a number of your remarks and also on certain observations I've made. For instance that clumping you thought was so awful in high school. You say that you even dreaded to walk into class. You see what you did? You dropped out of school, you gave up an education because of a clump, which as far as I know was practically non-existent! A little physical defect is what you have. Hardly noticeable even! Magnified thousands of times by imagination!

You know what my strong advice to you is? Think of yourself as *superior* in some way!

LAURA: In what way would I think?

JIM: Why, man alive, Laura! Just look about you a little. What do you see? A world full of common people! All of 'em born and all of 'em going to die!

Which of them has one-tenth of your good points! Or mine! Or anyone else's, as far as that goes – Gosh! Everybody excels in some one thing. Some in many!

[*Unconsciously glances at himself in the mirror.*]

All you've got to do is discover in *what!*
Take me, for instance.

[*He adjusts his tie at the mirror.*]

My interest happens to lie in electro-dynamics. I'm taking a course in radio engineering at night school, Laura, on top of a fairly responsible job at the warehouse. I'm taking that course and studying public speaking.

LAURA: Ohhhh.

JIM: Because I believe in the future of television!

[*Turning back to her.*]

I wish to be ready to go up right along with it. Therefore

I'm planning to get in on the ground floor. In fact I've already made the right connexions and all that remains is for the industry itself to get under way ! Full steam –

[*His eyes are starry.*]

Knowledge – Zzzzzp ! *Money* – Zzzzzzp ! – *Power!*
That's the cycle democracy is built on !

[*His attitude is convincingly dynamic.* LAURA *stares at him, even her shyness eclipsed in her absolute wonder. He suddenly grins.*]

I guess you think I think a lot of myself !

LAURA: No – o-o-o, I –

JIM: Now how about you? Isn't there something you take more interest in than anything else?

LAURA: Well, I do – as I said – have my – glass collection –

[*A peal of girlish laughter from the kitchen.*]

JIM: I'm not right sure I know what you're talking about. What kind of glass is it?

LAURA: Little articles of it, they're ornaments mostly !
Most of them are little animals made out of glass, the tiniest little animals in the world. Mother calls them a glass menagerie !
Here's an example of one, if you'd like to see it !
This one is one of the oldest. It's nearly thirteen.

[MUSIC: 'THE GLASS MENAGERIE'.
    He stretches out his hand.]

Oh, be careful – if you breathe, it breaks !

JIM: I'd better not take it. I'm pretty clumsy with things.

LAURA: Go on, I trust you with him !

[*Places it in his palm.*]

There now – you're holding him gently !

Hold him over the light, he loves the light! You see how the light shines through him?

JIM: It sure does shine!

LAURA: I shouldn't be partial, but he is my favourite one.

JIM: What kind of a thing is this one supposed to be?

LAURA: Haven't you noticed the single horn on his forehead?

JIM: A unicorn, huh?

LAURA: Mmmm-hmmm!

JIM: Unicorns, aren't they extinct in the modern world?

LAURA: I know!

JIM: Poor little fellow, he must feel sort of lonesome.

LAURA [*smiling*]: Well, if he does he doesn't complain about it. He stays on a shelf with some horses that don't have horns and all of them seem to get along nicely together.

JIM: How do you know?

LAURA [*lightly*]: I haven't heard any arguments among them!

JIM [*grinning*]: No arguments, huh? Well, that's a pretty good sign! Where shall I set him?

LAURA: Put him on the table. They all like a change of scenery once in a while!

JIM [*stretching*]: Well, well, well, well –
Look how big my shadow is when I stretch!

LAURA: Oh, oh, yes – it stretches across the ceiling!

JIM [*crossing to door*]: I think it's stopped raining. [*Opens fire-escape door.*] Where does the music come from?

LAURA: From the Paradise Dance Hall across the alley.

JIM: How about cutting the rug a little, Miss Wingfield?

LAURA: Oh –

JIM: Or is your programme filled up? Let me have a look at it. [*Grasps imaginary card.*] Why, every dance is taken! I'll just have to scratch some out. [WALTZ MUSIC: 'LA GOLONDRINA'.] Ahhh, a waltz! [*He executes some sweeping turns by himself then holds his arms toward* LAURA.]

LAURA [*breathlessly*]: I – can't dance!

JIM: There you go, that inferiority stuff!
   Come on, try!
LAURA: Oh, but I'd step on you!
JIM: I'm not made out of glass.
LAURA: How – how – how do we start?
JIM: Just leave it to me. You hold your arms out a little.
LAURA: Like this?
JIM: A little bit higher. Right. Now don't tighten up, that's
   the main thing about it – relax.
LAURA [*laughing breathlessly*]: It's hard not to.
   I'm afraid you can't budge me.
JIM: What do you bet I can't? [*He swings her into motion.*]
LAURA: Goodness, yes, you can!
JIM: Let yourself go, now, Laura, just let yourself go.
LAURA: I'm –
JIM: Come on!
LAURA: Trying!
JIM: Not so stiff – Easy does it!
LAURA: I know but I'm –
JIM: Loosen th' backbone! There now, that's a lot better.
LAURA: Am I?
JIM: Lots, lots better! [*He moves her about the room in a clumsy
   waltz.*]
LAURA: Oh, my!
JIM: Ha-ha!
LAURA: Oh, my goodness!
JIM: Ha-ha-ha! [*They suddenly bump into the table.* JIM *stops.*]
   What did we hit on?
LAURA: Table.
JIM: Did something fall off it? I think –
LAURA: Yes.
JIM: I hope that it wasn't the little glass horse with the horn!
LAURA: Yes.
JIM: Aw, aw, aw. Is it broken?
LAURA: Now it is just like all the other horses.
JIM: It's lost its –

LAURA: Horn!
It doesn't matter. Maybe it's a blessing in disguise.

JIM: You'll never forgive me. I bet that that was your favourite piece of glass.

LAURA: I don't have favourites much. It's no tragedy, Freckles. Glass breaks so easily. No matter how careful you are. The traffic jars the shelves and things fall off them.

JIM: Still I'm awfully sorry that I was the cause.

LAURA [*smiling*]: I'll just imagine he had an operation. The horn was removed to make him feel less – freakish!

[*They both laugh.*]

Now he will feel more at home with the other horses, the ones that don't have horns. . . .

JIM: Ha-ha, that's very funny!

[*Suddenly serious.*]

I'm glad to see that you have a sense of humour.
You know – you're – well – very different!
Surprisingly different from anyone else I know!

[*His voice becomes soft and hesitant with a genuine feeling.*]

Do you mind me telling you that?

[LAURA *is abashed beyond speech.*]

I mean it in a nice way . . .

[LAURA *nods shyly, looking away.*]

You make me feel sort of – I don't know how to put it!
I'm usually pretty good at expressing things, but –
This is something that I don't know how to say!

[LAURA *touches her throat and clears it – turns the broken unicorn in her hands.
Even softer.*]

Has anyone ever told you that you were pretty?

[PAUSE: MUSIC.
    LAURA *looks up slowly, with wonder, and shakes her head.*]

Well, you are! In a very different way from anyone else.
And all the nicer because of the difference, too.

[*His voice becomes low and husky.* LAURA *turns away, nearly
faint with the novelty of her emotions.*]

I wish that you were my sister. I'd teach you to have some
confidence in yourself. The different people are not like
other people, but being different is nothing to be ashamed
of. Because other people are not such wonderful people.
They're one hundred times one thousand. You're one
times one! They walk all over the earth. You just stay
here. They're common as – weeds, but – you – well,
you're – *Blue Roses!*

[IMAGE ON SCREEN: BLUE ROSES.
    MUSIC CHANGES.]

LAURA: But blue is wrong for – roses . . .
JIM: It's right for you! – You're – pretty!
LAURA: In what respect am I pretty?
JIM: In all respects – believe me! Your eyes – your hair –
are pretty! Your hands are pretty!

[*He catches hold of her hand.*]

You think I'm making this up because I'm invited to
dinner and have to be nice. Oh, I could do that! I could
put on an act for you, Laura, and say lots of things without being very sincere. But this time I am. I'm talking to
you sincerely. I happened to notice you had this inferiority complex that keeps you from feeling comfortable
with people. Somebody needs to build your confidence
up and make you proud instead of shy and turning away
and – blushing – Somebody – ought to –

Ought to – *kiss* you, Laura!

[*His hand slips slowly up her arm to her shoulder.*
    MUSIC SWELLS TUMULTUOUSLY.
    He suddenly turns her about and kisses her on the lips.
    When he releases her, LAURA *sinks on the sofa with a*
bright, dazed look.
    JIM *backs away and fishes in his pocket for a cigarette.*
    LEGEND ON SCREEN: 'SOUVENIR'.]

Stumble-john!

[*He lights the cigarette, avoiding her look.*
    There is a peal of girlish laughter from AMANDA *in the*
kitchen.
    LAURA *slowly raises and opens her hand. It still contains*
the little broken glass animal. She looks at it with a tender,
bewildered expression.]

Stumble-john! – Someone being stupid
I shouldn't have done that – That was way off the beam.
You don't smoke, do you?

[*She looks up, smiling, not hearing the question.*
    He sits beside her a little gingerly. She looks at him speech-
lessly – waiting.
    He coughs decorously and moves a little farther aside as he
considers the situation and senses her feelings, dimly, with per-
turbation.
    Gently.]

Would you – care for a – mint?

[*She doesn't seem to hear him but her look grows brighter*
even.]
Peppermint – Life-Saver?
My pocket's a regular drug store – wherever I go . . .

[*He pops a mint in his mouth. Then gulps and decides to make*
a clean breast of it. He speaks slowly and gingerly.]

Laura, you know, if I had a sister like you, I'd do the
same thing as Tom. I'd bring out fellows and – introduce
her to them. The right type of boys of a type to – appre-
ciate her.

Only – well – he made a mistake about me.

Maybe I've got no call to be saying this. That may not
have been the idea in having me over. But what if it was?
There's nothing wrong about that. The only trouble is
that in my case – I'm not in a situation to – do the right
thing.

I can't take down your number and say I'll phone.

I can't call up next week and – ask for a date.

I thought I had better explain the situation in case you –
misunderstand it and – hurt your feelings. . . .

> [*Pause.*
>   *Slowly, very slowly,* LAURA'*s look changes, her eyes re-
> turning slowly from his to the ornament in her palm.*
>   AMANDA *utters another gay laugh in the kitchen.*]

LAURA [*faintly*]: You – won't – call again?
JIM: No, Laura, I can't.

> [*He rises from the sofa.*]

As I was just explaining, I've – got strings on me.

Laura, I've – been going steady!

I go out all of the time with a girl named Betty. She's a
home-girl like you, and Catholic, and Irish, and in a great
many ways we – get along fine.

I met her last summer on a moonlight boat trip up the
river to Alton, on the *Majestic.*

Well – right away from the start it was – love!

> [LEGEND: 'LOVE!'
>   LAURA *sways slightly forward and grips the arm of the
> sofa. He fails to notice, now enrapt in his own comfortable
> being.*]

Being in love has made a new man of me!

[*Leaning stiffly forward, clutching the arm of the sofa,* LAURA *struggles visibly with her storm. But* JIM *is oblivious, she is a long way off.*]

The power of love is really pretty tremendous!
Love is something that – changes the whole world, Laura!

[*The storm abates a little and* LAURA *leans back. He notices her again.*]

It happened that Betty's aunt took sick, she got a wire and had to go to Centralia. So Tom – when he asked me to dinner – I naturally just accepted the invitation, not knowing that you – that he – that I –

[*He stops awkwardly.*]

Huh – I'm a stumble-john!

[*He flops back on the sofa.*
    The holy candles in the altar of LAURA'S *face have been snuffed out.*
    There is a look of almost infinite desolation.
    JIM *glances at her uneasily.*]

I wish that you would – say something. [*She bites her lip which was trembling and then bravely smiles. She opens her hand again on the broken glass ornament. Then she gently takes his hand and raises it level with her own. She carefully places the unicorn in the palm of his hand, then pushes his fingers closed upon it.*] What are you – doing that for? You want me to have him? Laura? [*She nods.*] What for?
LAURA: A – souvenir ...

[*She rises unsteadily and crouches beside the victrola to wind it up.*
    LEGEND ON SCREEN: 'THINGS HAVE A WAY OF TURNING OUT SO BADLY!'

OR IMAGE: GENTLEMAN CALLER WAVING
GOOD-BYE! – GAILY.

At this moment AMANDA *rushes brightly back in the
front room. She bears a pitcher of fruit punch in an old-
fashioned cut-glass pitcher and a plate of macaroons. The
plate has a gold border and poppies painted on it.*]

AMANDA: Well, well, well! Isn't the air delightful after
the shower? I've made you children a little liquid refresh-
ment.

   [*Turns gaily to the gentleman caller.*]

Jim, do you know that song about lemonade?
               'Lemonade, lemonade
               Made in the shade and stirred with a spade –
               Good enough for any old maid!'
JIM [*uneasily*]: Ha-ha! No – I never heard it.
AMANDA: Why, Laura! You look so serious!
JIM: We were having a serious conversation.
AMANDA: Good! Now you're better acquainted!
JIM [*uncertainly*]: Ha-ha! Yes.
AMANDA: You modern young people are much more
serious-minded than my generation. I was so gay as a
girl!
JIM: You haven't changed, Mrs Wingfield.
AMANDA: Tonight I'm rejuvenated! The gaiety of the
occasion, Mr O'Connor!

   [*She tosses her head with a peal of laughter. Spills lemonade.*]

Oooo! I'm baptizing myself!
JIM: Here – let me –
AMANDA [*setting the pitcher down*]: There now. I discovered
we had some maraschino cherries. I dumped them in,
juice and all!
JIM: You shouldn't have gone to that trouble, Mrs Wingfield.

AMANDA: Trouble, trouble? Why, it was loads of fun! Didn't you hear me cutting up in the kitchen? I bet your ears were burning! I told Tom how outdone with him I was for keeping you to himself so long a time! He should have brought you over much, much sooner! Well, now that you've found your way, I want you to be a very frequent caller! Not just occasional but all the time. Oh, we're going to have a lot of gay times together! I see them coming!

Mmm, just breathe that air! So fresh, and the moon's so pretty!

I'll skip back out – I know where my place is when young folks are having a – serious conversation!

JIM: Oh, don't go out, Mrs Wingfield. The fact of the matter is I've got to be going.

AMANDA: Going, now? You're joking! Why, it's only the shank of the evening, Mr O'Connor!

JIM: Well, you know how it is.

AMANDA: You mean you're a young working man and have to keep working men's hours. We'll let you off early tonight.

But only on the condition that next time you stay later. What's the best night for you? Isn't Saturday night the best night for you working men?

JIM: I have a couple of time-clocks to punch, Mrs Wingfield. One at morning, another one at night!

AMANDA: My, but you *are* ambitious! You work at night, too?

JIM: No, Ma'am, not work but – Betty! [*He crosses deliberately to pick up his hat. The band at the Paradise Dance Hall goes into a tender waltz.*]

AMANDA: Betty? Betty? Who's – Betty!

[*There is an ominous cracking sound in the sky.*]

JIM: Oh, just a girl. The girl I go steady with! [*He smiles charmingly. The sky falls.*]

[LEGEND: 'THE SKY FALLS'.]

AMANDA [*a long-drawn exhalation*]: Ohhhh. ... Is it a serious romance, Mr O'Connor?

JIM: We're going to be married the second Sunday in June.

AMANDA: Ohhhh – how nice!

Tom didn't mention that you were engaged to be married.

JIM: The cat's not out of the bag at the warehouse yet. You know how they are. They call you Romeo and stuff like that.

[*He stops at the oval mirror to put on his hat. He carefully shapes the brim and the crown to give a discreetly dashing effect.*]

It's been a wonderful evening, Mrs Wingfield. I guess this is what they mean by Southern hospitality.

AMANDA: It really wasn't anything at all.

JIM: I hope it don't seem like I'm rushing off. But I promised Betty I'd pick her up at the Wabash depot, an' by the time I get my jalopy down there her train'll be in. Some women are pretty upset if you keep 'em waiting.

AMANDA: Yes, I know – The tyranny of women!

[*Extends her hand.*]

Good-bye, Mr O'Connor.

I wish you luck – and happiness – and success! All three of them, and so does Laura! – Don't you, Laura?

LAURA: Yes!

JIM [*taking her hand*]: Good-bye, Laura. I'm certainly going to treasure that souvenir. And don't you forget the good advice I gave you.

[*Raises his voice to a cheery shout.*]

So long, Shakespeare!

Thanks again, ladies – Good night!

[*He grins and ducks jauntily out.*]

Still bravely grimacing, AMANDA *closes the door on the gentleman caller. Then she turns back to the room with a puzzled expression. She and* LAURA *don't dare face each other.* LAURA *crouches beside the victrola to wind it.*]

AMANDA [*faintly*]: Things have a way of turning out so badly.

I don't believe that I would play the victrola.

Well, well – well –

Our gentleman caller was engaged to be married!

Tom!

TOM [*from back*]: Yes, Mother?

AMANDA: Come in here a minute. I want to tell you something awfully funny.

TOM [*enters with macaroon and a glass of lemonade*]: Has the gentleman caller gotten away already?

AMANDA: The gentleman caller has made an early departure. What a wonderful joke you played on us!

TOM: How do you mean?

AMANDA: You didn't mention that he was engaged to be married.

TOM: Jim? Engaged?

AMANDA: That's what he just informed us.

TOM: I'll be jiggered! I didn't know about that.

AMANDA: That seems very peculiar.

TOM: What's peculiar about it?

AMANDA: Didn't you call him your best friend down at the warehouse?

TOM: He is, but how did I know?

AMANDA: It seems extremely peculiar that you wouldn't know your best friend was going to be married!

TOM: The warehouse is where I work, not where I know things about people!

AMANDA: You don't know things anywhere! You live in a dream; you manufacture illusions!

[*He crosses to door.*]

Where are you going?

TOM: I'm going to the movies.

AMANDA: That's right, now that you've had us make such
fools of ourselves. The effort, the preparations, all the
expense! The new floor lamp, the rug, the clothes for
Laura! All for what? To entertain some other girl's
fiancé! Go to the movies, go! Don't think about us, a
mother deserted, an unmarried sister who's crippled and
has no job! Don't let anything interfere with your selfish
pleasure! Just go, go, go – to the movies!

TOM: All right, I will! The more you shout about my
selfishness to me the quicker I'll go, and I won't go to the
movies!

AMANDA: Go, then! Then go to the moon – you selfish
dreamer!

[TOM *smashes his glass on the floor. He plunges out on the
fire-escape, slamming the door.* LAURA *screams – cut by door.*

Dance-hall music up. TOM *goes to the rail and grips it
desperately, lifting his face in the chill white moonlight penetrating the narrow abyss of the alley.*

LEGEND ON SCREEN: 'AND SO GOOD-BYE . . .'

TOM'S *closing speech is timed with the interior pantomime.
The interior scene is played as though viewed through sound-
proof glass.* AMANDA *appears to be making a comforting
speech to* LAURA *who is huddled upon the sofa. Now that we
cannot hear the mother's speech, her silliness is gone and she
has dignity and tragic beauty.* LAURA'S *dark hair hides her
face until at the end of the speech she lifts it to smile at her
mother.* AMANDA'S *gestures are slow and graceful, almost
dancelike, as she comforts the daughter. At the end of her speech
she glances a moment at the father's picture – then withdraws
through the portières. At the close of* TOM'S *speech,* LAURA
blows out the candles, ending the play.]

TOM: I didn't go to the moon, I went much further – for time is the longest distance between two places –

Not long after that I was fired for writing a poem on the lid of a shoebox.

I left Saint Louis. I descended the steps of this fire-escape for a last time and followed, from then on, in my father's footsteps, attempting to find in motion what was lost in space – I travelled around a great deal. The cities swept about me like dead leaves, leaves that were brightly coloured but torn away from the branches.

I would have stopped, but I was pursued by something.

It always came upon me unawares, taking me altogether by surprise. Perhaps it was a familiar bit of music. Perhaps it was only a piece of transparent glass –

Perhaps I am walking along a street at night, in some strange city, before I have found companions. I pass the lighted window of a shop where perfume is sold. The window is filled with pieces of coloured glass, tiny transparent bottles in delicate colours, like bits of a shattered rainbow.

Then all at once my sister touches my shoulder. I turn around and look into her eyes . . .

Oh, Laura, Laura, I tried to leave you behind me, but I am more faithful than I intended to be!

I reach for a cigarette, I cross the street, I run into the movies or a bar, I buy a drink, I speak to the nearest stranger – anything that can blow your candles out!

[LAURA *bends over the candles.*]

– for nowadays the world is lit by lightning! Blow out your candles, Laura – and so good-bye. . . .

[*She blows the candles out.*]

THE SCENE DISSOLVES

Williams presents America as a horrible country – presents characters as a family living in a horrible block of building leading a horrible life

READ MORE IN PENGUIN

In every corner of the world, on every subject under the sun, Penguin represents quality and variety – the very best in publishing today.

For complete information about books available from Penguin – including Puffins, Penguin Classics and Arkana – and how to order them, write to us at the appropriate address below. Please note that for copyright reasons the selection of books varies from country to country.

In the United Kingdom: Please write to *Dept. EP, Penguin Books Ltd, Bath Road, Harmondsworth, West Drayton, Middlesex UB7 ODA*

In the United States: Please write to *Consumer Sales, Penguin Putnam Inc., P.O. Box 999, Dept. 17109, Bergenfield, New Jersey 07621-0120.* VISA and MasterCard holders call 1-800-253-6476 to order Penguin titles

In Canada: Please write to *Penguin Books Canada Ltd, 10 Alcorn Avenue, Suite 300, Toronto, Ontario M4V 3B2*

In Australia: Please write to *Penguin Books Australia Ltd, P.O. Box 257, Ringwood, Victoria 3134*

In New Zealand: Please write to *Penguin Books (NZ) Ltd, Private Bag 102902, North Shore Mail Centre, Auckland 10*

In India: Please write to *Penguin Books India Pvt Ltd, 210 Chiranjiv Tower, 43 Nehru Place, New Delhi 110 019*

In the Netherlands: Please write to *Penguin Books Netherlands bv, Postbus 3507, NL-1001 AH Amsterdam*

In Germany: Please write to *Penguin Books Deutschland GmbH, Metzlerstrasse 26, 60594 Frankfurt am Main*

In Spain: Please write to *Penguin Books S. A., Bravo Murillo 19, 1° B, 28015 Madrid*

In Italy: Please write to *Penguin Italia s.r.l., Via Benedetto Croce 2, 20094 Corsico, Milano*

In France: Please write to *Penguin France, Le Carré Wilson, 62 rue Benjamin Baillaud, 31500 Toulouse*

In Japan: Please write to *Penguin Books Japan Ltd, Kaneko Building, 2-3-25 Koraku, Bunkyo-Ku, Tokyo 112*

In South Africa: Please write to *Penguin Books South Africa (Pty) Ltd, Private Bag X14, Parkview, 2122 Johannesburg*

BY THE SAME AUTHOR

Cat on a Hot Tin Roof and Other Plays

'Williams has a long reach and a genuinely dramatic imagination ... He is constantly pressing his own limits. He creates shows, as all of us must, but he possesses the restless inconsolability with his solutions which is inevitable in a genuine writer' – Arthur Miller

Cat on a Hot Tin Roof: in the heart of the American South, a family is imprisoned in the midst of untold richness by greed, envy and crippling self-deception.

The Milk Train Doesn't Stop Here Anymore: An ageing American actress dictates her memoirs in a luxurious Mediterranean retreat.

The Night of the Iguana: A lusty hotel proprietor, a defrocked clergyman, an old poet and a family of beer-drinking Nazis are brought together in Mexico.

Also published:

Baby Doll and Other Plays
The Rose Tattoo and Other Plays
A Street Car Named Desire and Other Plays
Period of Adjustment and Other Plays